THE AMERICAN SYMPHONY ORCHESTRA

THE
AMERICAN
SYMPHONY
ORCHESTRA

Edited by HENRY SWOBODA

BASIC BOOKS, INC., PUBLISHERS
New York   *London*

The Authors

MAURICE ABRAVANEL is permanent Conductor of the Utah Symphony Orchestra. He came to Salt Lake City in 1947 and in the twenty years that followed put this community orchestra on the national map as one of America's better orchestras. An invitation to the Athens Festival 1966 and a European tour have betokened this accomplishment. He also directs the Music Academy of the West in Santa Barbara, California.

WILFRED C. BAIN is Dean of the School of Music at Indiana University and for the past twenty years has been leader of this world-important school. Dean Bain has served in high positions in the National Association of the Schools of Music, the Music Teacher's Association, The Metropolitan Opera Council, and the Berkshire Center Committee, to name a few.

JULIUS BLOOM is Executive Director of the Carnegie Hall Corporation and Director of Concerts and Lectures for Rutgers University. It was as Executive Director of the National Institute of Music that he was appointed to his present positions with the Carnegie Hall Corporation and as cultural counselor to both Newark and New York City.

MARTIN BOOKSPAN is Director of Recorded Music for Station WQXR in New York City. In this important post he supervises the programing of WQXR's recorded classical music broadcasts to the tune of eighty hours a week. In 1954, he became Radio, Television, and Recordings Coordinator for the Boston Symphony Orchestra, at the same time serving as Director of Serious Music Programs for station WBZ in Boston. He continues to offer special programs and commentaries vis-à-vis the Boston Orchestra as one of his many musical specials for station WQXR.

AARON COPLAND is one of America's outstanding composers, indeed a leading musical figure in the Western Hemisphere. A writer and lecturer of great lucidity, he has toured the world in recent years, alternating as conductor, pianist, and speaker—but always the leading exponent of contemporary American music. His books *What to Listen for in Music* and *Music and Imagination* are classics. He is a much honored member of the National Institute of Arts and Letters and winner of the Presidential Medal of Freedom.

CURTIS DAVIS is Director of Cultural Programs for The National Educational Television and Radio Center. As an Associate Director for Film of the Council for the Humanities he designed the first twelve films of a high school television course in the humanities. Since 1959 he has been associated with NET, first as Program Associate, then as Executive Producer and Cultural Programs Director.

ALFRED V. FRANKENSTEIN is the Art Critic and former Music Critic of the *San Francisco Chronicle*. A frequent and outstanding performer in the Salzburg Seminar in American Studies, he has also taught at Harvard University, University of Hawaii, Stanford University, The University of Chicago, and Free University of Berlin. Two forthcoming books are *A Modern Guide to Symphonic Music* and *Pictures at an Exhibition and Other Studies in the Arts*. His *After the Hunt* (1953) appeared in a new edition in 1966.

HOWARD HANSON is Director of the Institute of American Music and former Director of the Eastman School of Music. His name is a by-word in American musical circles as spokesman for modern American music. Winner of the Prix de Rome in 1921, he was invited directly to be Director of the Eastman School of Music, which position he held for more than forty years. He is a talented conductor and has taken his own orchestra on many tours.

PAUL HUME has been Music Editor of *The Washington Post* since 1947. He is also Professor of Music and Director of the Glee Club of Georgetown University. His candid reviews of artistic performances in the United States Capital have attracted wide attention. Among his books is *Catholic Church Music* (1956).

LEON KIRCHNER is Walter Bigelow Rosen Professor of Music at Harvard University. A man acclaimed for his composing, conducting, and pianism, he today mixes lively performances of the three arts with the more quiet profession of teaching. In 1962, ten years after his appointment to Harvard, he was elected to the National Institute of Arts and Letters and to the Academy of Arts and Science. He has written a piano concerto, a concerto for violin, cello, 10 winds, and percussion; several string quartets; songs; and scenes for an opera.

TIBERIUS KLAUSNER is Concertmaster of the Kansas City Philharmonic Orchestra and founder and First Violinist of the Klausner String Quartet. He has performed regularly in symphony performances and solo concerti with the Kansas City Philharmonic. He also teaches and performs as soloist with other orchestras.

JOSEF KRIPS is Conductor and Musical Director of The San Francisco Symphony Orchestra. He began his career of conducting at the Vienna Volksoper in 1921. From the Volksoper he moved to various conducting assignments, returning to the Staatsoper of Vienna in 1933, and re-emerged from the ruins of war as the chief architect of Austria's musical renaissance. Invitations from the London Symphony Orchestra and Buffalo Symphony Orchestra acquainted others with Dr. Krips's musical authority, and San Francisco and international prominence became his destinations.

ERICH LEINSDORF is Musical Director and Conductor of the Boston Symphony Orchestra. He first rose to prominence in 1934 as assistant to Bruno Walter and Arturo Toscanini at the Salzburg Festival. Responsible for bringing the Rochester Philharmonic into the national limelight in the years 1947 to 1956, he was invited to the directorship of the Metropolitan Opera Company and the Boston Symphony Orchestra in 1962.

WALTER PISTON is an eminent composer, now Professor Emeritus of Music at Harvard University. Orchestral and chamber music mark his musical output, works worthy of a Pulitzer Prize in 1948. His published musicological studies deal with harmony, counterpoint, harmonic analysis, and orchestration. Mr. Piston is a member of the National Institute of Arts and Letters, the American Academy of Arts and Sciences, and the American Academy of Arts and Letters.

SAMUEL R. ROSENBAUM, member of USIA's Music Advisory Panel, has served as Impartial Trustee of The Recording Industries Trust Funds since 1948. For years he has been on the board of the Philadelphia Orchestra Association, Robin Hood Dell, and the Composer's Forum. In recent years he has chaired the executive committee of the Inter-American Music Festival.

MAX RUDOLF is Music Director and Conductor of the Cincinnati Symphony Orchestra. This fifth oldest of America's symphony orchestras (founded 1895) has recently returned from a world tour under Department of State auspices that took it from Athens to Seoul. From 1950 to 1955 he was artistic administrator of the Metropolitan Opera Association in New York, being invited to head Cincinnati's prestigious institution in 1958. Author of *The Grammar of Conducting,* he also taught in the Ford Foundation project for conductors at Peabody Conservatory in Baltimore.

WILLIAM SCHUMAN is President of the Lincoln Center for the Performing Arts in New York City. Dr. Schuman is known both as composer and educator. His works for orchestra include eight symphonies; he has composed choral works, band works, chamber music and scores for films. He was President of the Juilliard School of Music and is a Fellow of the National Institute of Arts and Letters, and an honorary member of the Royal Academy of Music.

NICOLAS SLONIMSKY is lecturer on Music at the University of California, Los Angeles. In 1927 he founded the Chamber Orchestra of Boston and subsequently conducted programs of new American music in Paris, Berlin, Budapest, etc. (and gave world premiers of orchestral works by Charles Ives, Henry Cowell, Edgar Varèse, Carlos Chávez, and others). Among his most important musicological publications are *Music since 1900, The Road to Music,* and *Lexicon of Musical Invective.*

LEOPOLD STOKOWSKI is Music Director and Conductor of the American Symphony Orchestra. In 1912 he began his association as conductor of the Philadelphia Orchestra, which was to last twenty-six years. He began in those years experiments with seating and acoustics. After Philadelphia, other conductorships came his way, but he has been most interested in creating new orchestras, most recently the American Symphony Orchestra, which employs talented young persons regardless of background.

HENRY SWOBODA, recently in resident at Harvard University and the University of Texas, is known through his symphonic recordings of the classical and contemporary repertoire. He has toured with leading orchestras in Europe and Latin America. The State Department has used his services on several occasions as goodwill ambassador within its cultural program.

HELEN M. THOMPSON is Executive Vice President of the American Symphony Orchestra League. She brings to her position a compassionate dedication to the orchestra musician and his institutional place in American life. During Mrs. Thompson's tenure, the symphony orchestra has come of age as an artistic and legal entity.

G. WALLACE WOODWORTH is Professor of Music at Harvard University. He is a patron of musical growth in the Cambridge area. His major opus, *The World of Music,* was published in 1964. Dr. Woodworth is a fellow of the American Academy of Arts and Sciences and a member of the American Musicological Society.

Preface

Since there is, to my knowledge, no contemporary handbook available describing the unusual evolution of symphonic life in America within the recent past, I enthusiastically accepted the assignment to coordinate a series of lectures and interviews on the American symphony orchestra for the Forum program of the Voice of America. This was an opportunity to acquaint the world at large with an important segment of our cultural life. Within its own limited frame of reference, this résumé may perhaps shed some light on certain situations the "outsider" not actually involved in these happenings may find somewhat puzzling. We would also like to believe that through these pages interest in our symphonic organizations, large and small, may be stimulated.

This book does not pretend to offer an encyclopedic presentation of the American symphony orchestra; it should rather be regarded, however, as a selective overview of achievements, shortcomings, and trends, as well as cultural and financial aspects of our symphonic life, evaluated and discussed by personalities qualified to deal with such issues. We have tried to give the reader as honest and as candid a picture of today's orchestral scene as possible.

My choice of participants may easily be challenged and, in the last analysis, this delicate question can only be answered on the basis of individual preference. Since, obviously, duplications could hardly be avoided, we would like to assume that the reader may find it interesting to compare varying opinions on the same subject as they are expressed by seasoned observers.

It took all of two years to assemble the required material, and during the time elapsed between the inception and completion of this series drastic changes on our symphonic scene have taken shape. New legislation favoring support of the arts was enacted, and an $85 million grant was established by the Ford Foundation for our orchestras. Though, in certain instances, matching of these latter funds may create problems, these two innovations can doubtless be regarded as milestones on the road toward a brighter future of symphonic music in the United States.

Much has been said and written about our "great" orchestras, and not only the interested listener but the public at large is conscious of their glamorous existence. If some of these organizations are mentioned here, it is not because we want to dwell on facts long known and established. We intend rather to point to the relationships of these orchestras to regional expansion. Here we are more directly concerned with what could be called the grass-roots development within the last two decades. The foreigner, even the European, well informed as he may be on musical matters in his own country, has at best a vague conception about the history and organization of the American symphony orchestra. Perhaps, to some, aspects of this fascinating development may come as a surprise.

The reader will discover the exquisitely complex interrelationship of governmental and private assistance to the arts as established here. He may marvel at the tremendous moral and financial effort put forward by corporations, foundations, and private individuals in support of some of our symphonic organizations. It has been only recently that government (federal and state) has taken action to share financial responsibility for the arts. We still have a long way to go and there may be rough sailing ahead for some of our orchestral groups, but the active interest, good will, and generosity of private citizens, coupled with financial assistance assured by legislation, augurs well for the future of the American symphony orchestra, as we turn the page to start on a new chapter of musical history in America.

The musician's language is music, and he prefers to express his thoughts through performing or composing or a combination of both, rather than by writing about his profession and related issues. Being aware of this reluctance, I am most grateful to our participants who so generously contributed their time in preparing this book, time some of them may have felt could have been spent more felicitously by just making music.

My sincerest thanks to all our collaborators who by their ever-present willingness to amplify their comments kept pace with day-to-day happenings on our symphonic scene. Many thanks also to my friend, Theodore A. Wertime, Forum Editor of the Voice of America, for his faithful cooperation and valuable advice, and to his assistant, Miss Joy MacFadyen.

La Tour de Peilz   HENRY SWOBODA
May 1967

Contents

THE AMERICAN SYMPHONY ORCHESTRA

1 AMERICANISM IN AMERICAN SYMPHONIC MUSIC

Nicolas Slonimsky

American ideals in American music constitute a large subject, for America is no longer a secondary nation in the world of music. Early in this century American music was to all intents and purposes a German colony, and American composers followed faithfully the precepts of Mendelssohn, Schumann, and Wagner. After World War I the German influence was broken. Soon new composers of genuine talent arose in this land.

Perhaps the most spectacular appearance was that of Charles Ives, who died in 1954 at the age of eighty and who was practically unknown until the last fifteen years of his life. Charles Ives created the type of American music the like of which had never existed and which is enormously difficult to perform. Someone asked Charles Ives why he didn't write a popular type of music that everyone could play and enjoy. "I can't," he replied, "I hear something else." The "something else" was an extraordinary world of true American music, based on dance rhythms of the American countryside, religious hymns he heard in church as a child in Connecticut, and popular American ballads. In the music of Ives these elements are combined into something uniquely individual and yet truly national. He believed that national music must be personal in order to become universal. Music, he said, is personal in the daytime, very often national at twilight, and becomes universal at midnight. Every note of

3

his music is American, but the treatment of this music is of the new century, perhaps of the centuries to come. He anticipated many modern usages that go by such terms as polytonality, atonality, and polyrhythms. His symphonic suite *Three Places in New England* is particularly remarkable in this respect. The music represents America in action. In the second movement two marching bands play the same march at different tempi. When I conducted the first performance of this work—some thirty years after it was written—I had to develop a special type of conducting, by beating four bars with my left hand against three bars with my right hand, in order to represent these two marching bands. The Fourth Symphony by Ives is without doubt the most complex work of the century. When its first complete performance was given in New York in April 1965, three conductors were necessary to coordinate its musical ingredients. And yet this music is derived from simple melodic ideas, including echoes of nineteenth-century ballads. Every work of Charles Ives is American in some way. In his *Concord Sonata* for piano, Charles Ives gives musical interpretations of four great personalities of American literature: Emerson, the essayist and poet; the Alcotts, the family of novelists; Thoreau, the philosopher of individualism who lived in a hut he built for himself at Walden Pond; and Hawthorne, the writer of American tales. In one of these movements Charles Ives uses a special effect in piano sonority. He instructs the pianist to place a wooden block on the keys without sounding the notes, so that they will reverberate when a related tone is struck in the harmonic series. The effect is virtually identical with tone clusters, developed by an American composer of the younger generation, Henry Cowell. Charles Ives is regarded as a supreme genius of American music, and his music is beginning to penetrate to Europe.

The first American composer of stature was Edward MacDowell, a highly civilized musician. He wrote beautiful pieces with American content. But MacDowell's music was intrinsically

4

European, with American ideas superimposed on its structure. Ives was only thirteen years younger than MacDowell, but this interval of time spanned an era. The difference is tremendous, for Ives completely disregarded the previous evolution of music and started out on something totally new. He anticipated forms of expression unimaginable in his time. It was not until a few years before his death that his music received recognition. When a Pulitzer Prize was awarded to him, he was unimpressed. "Prizes are for schoolboys," he said, "and I am no longer a schoolboy." He was not interested in worldly rewards, for he was a world in himself.

Let us now consider American composers of a younger generation. Among them Roy Harris is perhaps the most American in his music. He was born in 1898, on February 12, Lincoln's Birthday, in Lincoln County in Oklahoma. This coincidental connection with Lincoln became of symbolic significance in his career. He started to compose rather late in life. He went to Paris to study with the famous teacher Nadia Boulanger. But his music was never Parisianized. It spoke the tonal language of the wide-open spaces of the West where he was brought up. He developed his own technique of composition. Without actual quotations from American folk songs, Harris invented his own profoundly American style.

Quite different from the music of Charles Ives and Roy Harris is the creation of George Antheil, who was born in 1900 and died in 1959. The musical portrait of America that he painted in his music was the America of the machine age. In his youth he composed a *Mechanical Ballet* (*Ballet mécanique*), which included airplane propellers in its orchestration. When it was first performed in New York in 1927, it produced a sensation. At that time noise on the concert stage was still something new. But when Antheil's *Mechanical Ballet* was revived a few years ago it sounded like a period piece. Nobody could be impressed by airplane propellers in the jet age. But George Antheil retains his place in American music as the first composer of the avant-garde. He made his career in France while the French composer Edgar Varèse (1883–1965) was composing machine music in America. Varèse's *Ionization,* written for percussion instruments and two sirens, marked an epoch in music history. His great symphonic panoramas of sound have greatly influenced the development of musical composition in America.

Twentieth-century America produced a new medium of national self-expression—jazz—which had its fertile proliferation around the world. Modern American composers felt the influence of this powerful type of national music. Perhaps the most important symphonic composition in the jazz idiom was the Piano Concerto by Aaron Copland. When he played this concerto with the Boston Symphony Orchestra in 1927, the audience was profoundly shocked by this irruption of syncopated rhythms in dignified Symphony Hall. But Copland never intended to shock the bourgeoisie. After the Piano Concerto he went on to compose American music of deep significance in an individual modern idiom. Many of his works refer to the American scene. His remarkable symphonic work *A Lincoln Portrait,* with a narrator reciting words from Lincoln's speeches, has become a classic of American music. Aaron Copland is also adept in writing music for the stage; his ballets enjoy popular success.

Henry Cowell (1897–1965), of the same generation as Harris and Copland, began his career as an ultra-modernist. He invented the method of playing piano with forearms and elbows, and contributed the expression "tone cluster" to musical terminology. The spectacle of a pianist hitting the keyboard in such a way produced the expected shock. But Henry Cowell soon moved away from such external modernism and began writing works imbued with folksong elements, not only those of America but of the whole world.

In the second half of the twentieth century, the American avant-garde made further strides into the future. John Cage, who studied with Cowell, introduced the concept of "random music," in which the element of chance is as important as conscious composition. In order to produce new sonorities, he placed all kinds of objects on the strings of the grand piano—screws and bolts, copper coins and rubber bands—and called the result a "prepared piano." Among his works is the *Imaginary Landscape* for twelve radios, dialed according to a score indicating the prescribed wave lengths. The result is a fantasy of unrelated bits of music, speech, and static. The ultimate in his desire for novelty is a piece for silent piano, during which no intentional sounds are produced. The pianist sits at the keyboard and plays nothing.

On the other side of the American musical spectrum we find Walter Piston. Born in 1894, he represents the spirit of classical modernism. The formal perfection of his symphonies and the mastery of his counterpoint are rarely equaled. But his Americanism is of an abstract nature. He does not write programmatic music and does not attempt to shape his melodies and rhythms according to the inflection of American folk songs. He once said that American music can be written in the Boston Atheneum, among books, in the atmosphere of old culture. By virtue of being written in an American environment, this music is bound to assume a national flavor.

Romantic music is represented in America by Howard Hanson, who was born of Swedish parents in 1896, and Samuel Barber, born in 1910. Howard Hanson is quite outspoken in his allegiance; one of his symphonies bears the subtitle *Romantic*. Although the style of his music is cosmopolitan, he selected a subject from American history for his opera *Merrymount*. The romanticism of Samuel Barber has a rhapsodic quality. But he is not averse to applying the most complex harmonies and rhythms of modern music. His piano concerto is a virtuoso piece of the greatest difficulty, but it remains basically romantic in essence.

A close contemporary of Samuel Barber is William Schuman,

7

who was born in 1910. He is distinguished mainly as a symphonist. His works are set in classical form, but American melodic turns and phrases are often discernible in his music. He is also a capable educator and administrator. At present he occupies the highly important post of president of Lincoln Center of the Performing Arts in New York City.

The name of Roger Sessions should be mentioned. He enjoys great respect among American composers as a master of the craft of composition. His music presents great difficulties for performance, but his writing is almost classical in the clarity of its structure. Roger Sessions was born in 1896, as was Virgil Thomson, but no two composers could be more different. Virgil Thomson writes music which is tantalizingly simple in its harmony and rhythms but sophisticated in the extreme and demands concentrated attention for the appreciation of finer points. His most famous work is the opera *Four Saints in Three Acts,* to the text by the celebrated American writer Gertrude Stein. (Actually, there are more than a dozen saints in it, and it has four acts, not three.) Another opera, *The Mother of Us All,* depicts in surrealistic tones the career of the famous American suffragist Susan B. Anthony who fought for women's right to vote.

The name of George Gershwin is universally known for his brilliant and profoundly American score *Rhapsody in Blue.* He died in 1937 at the age of thirty-eight, but in his brief lifetime he succeeded in bridging the gap between popular and serious music. His folk opera *Porgy and Bess* and his many songs are perennial favorites with audiences in America and abroad.

Grand opera is not an American art. In Europe there are opera houses in every little town, but in America there are very few. Perhaps this is the reason why American composers rarely turn to operatic composition. It is a paradox that the most successful composer of American operas is Gian Carlo Menotti, an Italian-born musician who received his education in America. He writes his own librettos in English, and his expressive talent as a dramatist fully equals his musical gifts. His operas are brief, but effective; among them, *The Medium*, *The Consul*, and the Christmas fairy tale *Amahl and the Night Visitors* have become part of American operatic repertory.

A celebrated figure on the American scene is Leonard Bernstein. As conductor and musical director of the New York Philharmonic, he occupies one of the most important positions in the world of music. As a composer, he has written many symphonic works typically American in content. But he also is the creator of several brilliant musical comedies. Among his stage works, *West Side Story* is a classic in its genre. Bernstein is indeed a unique phenomenon in the versatility and effectiveness of his musical gifts.

2 FIFTY YEARS OF THE AMERICAN SYMPHONY ORCHESTRA: PERSONAL VIGNETTES

Walter Piston and G. Wallace Woodworth

G. WALLACE WOODWORTH: Walter Piston and I are going to discuss the American symphony orchestra, using the Boston Symphony Orchestra as centerpiece. Professor Piston has known the Boston Symphony for more than forty years.

First let me give a little background on the history of symphony orchestras in the United States. Curiously enough, the oldest American orchestra with a continuous history covering the period from the early nineteenth century to today is the Harvard University Symphony Orchestra, as it is now called, or the Pierian Sodality of 1808, as it was called in 1808 when it was founded. Of course, one of the great developers of symphonic music in the United States was Theodore Thomas, who had a traveling orchestra and was later the founder of the Chicago Symphony.

The Boston Symphony Orchestra dates back to 1881. It grew out of an orchestra called the Germania Orchestra, which was sponsored by the Harvard Musical Association, an association of graduates quite distinct from the Pierian Sodality. The Boston Symphony Orchestra was founded by Colonel Henry Lee Higginson. He was the sole supporter of it, and he paid its annual deficits for many years. The first conductor was George Henschel, an English singer, and, following him, the conductors for a good many years were Germans. I think Professor Piston remembers

Karl Muck and perhaps he will say something about the orchestra from the time of Muck to the present day.

WALTER PISTON: As a composer and also as a musician growing up, I had always had a very close relationship with the Boston Symphony, and as a student I used to stand in line to get in for twenty-five cents.

MR. WOODWORTH: So did I.

MR. PISTON: I think that a special discount for students is still given, although they don't make as many seats available now.

MR. WOODWORTH: Nor is the price twenty-five cents; it is sixty cents now. But a large block of seats is still reserved for students and other music lovers.

MR. PISTON: I think the Boston Symphony has been probably the greatest influence in my life as a composer. It happens that I have a preference for composing for a symphony orchestra; otherwise the association wouldn't have been so important. It occurs to me that they have played twenty first performances of my works. I have been so close to them that when I wrote the program notes about my Sixth Symphony I could hear the orchestra playing it as I composed it. I even went so far as to say I could almost hear the oboe playing the melody I was writing, so I picked up the notes he played and put them down. By the way, I was interested that you brought in the Pierian Sodality, since I conducted that orchestra when I was a student at Harvard. I learned a great deal about the orchestra from that experience because, as you know, one had to teach the players how to bow and how to phrase.

MR. WOODWORTH: This was in the late twenties and early thirties. I think Nicolas Slonimsky served as conductor between your term and mine. Walter, would you tell us something about the development of the orchestral techniques of the Boston Symphony? It had a long period of German domination and German technique which finally came to an end. You say you remember Muck. I first began to hear the Symphony when Pierre Monteux was conductor. He had been preceded by Henri Rabaud, who only conducted for one season. The great French tradition was continued by Sergey Koussevitzky and Charles Munch. And now we have Erich Leinsdorf. What about the development of the orchestra itself?

MR. PISTON: Well, of course, one likes to think that everything is getting better all the time. I am not entirely sure that it is a matter of technique. It is a matter of musical experience, which, it seems to me, has had its influence on the orchestra. These different conductors, of course, had their own ideas about programs and doing new works. It is by performing new works, it seems to me, that the technique is most brought to the fore. There is another important factor, and that is that nowadays there is very little rehearsal time. There are so many concerts and so little time to prepare them. The concerts I heard with Karl Muck were so perfect because they were rehearsed all week and then played on Friday and Saturday, whereas now very often there is no rehearsal until Wednesday, and there is just one run-through on Wednesday and two on Thursday. I might say that it is to the great credit of the orchestra's players and the conductor as well that the performances seem to have the same kind of perfection and skill that they had in the early days.

MR. WOODWORTH: The Boston Symphony has been abroad, in western Europe and Russia, and has played in the Far East. One always wonders what the effect is of that sort of international, or cultural exchange, as it is called. I remember your mentioning some surprising communication you received from Prague. This did not relate so much to the Boston Symphony as to your own music being played abroad; but certainly the Boston Symphony Orchestra tours and the trips by other American orchestras have done something to let the rest of the world know what one facet of American music is like. In the past few years, we have been having an increasing number of reciprocal visits from foreign orchestras here in the United States. I think our readers would be interested to learn about the two communications from Prague.

MR. PISTON: Well, that was very gratifying to me. I received a nice letter accompanied by programs and big posters about a performance of my viola concerto in Prague. To begin with, I wonder where they could have gotten the music. And I also wonder why they should happen to want to play this particular piece. Sometime after this I got an equally nice communication from a woodwind group in Prague that had performed my wind quintet. I also had pleasant and fruitful contacts with some Russian composers who came here. They took back my music with them and it is being played in Russia a good deal. I am always delighted to find that music has such a power of communication with people with whom we have so little contact. This was especially marked in my experience with the Prague performances because the woodwind quintet sent me a tape recording, but before I opened it I said: "Well, this will be a real test of the hands-across-the-sea aspect of the art of music because this is a performance to which I contributed nothing but the notes and because they do not know me, my personality, or anything else about me." I was amazed when I played the tape because the concerto was performed in exactly the way I would like it to be performed, and, in fact, it was closer to my ideal than many performances I have had in this country by musicians whom I know very well. This pleased me very much because I do believe that there is some kind of universal language in the art of music. It was very encouraging in many ways.

MR. WOODWORTH: We have been discussing Boston and the Boston Symphony. Maybe we ought to broaden the field and consider the whole United States. I believe that books about American orchestral music are apt to classify the orchestras as A, B, or C. There are, let us say, six or eight or ten Class A orchestras, like the New York Philharmonic, the Chicago Orchestra, the Philadelphia, Boston, and Cleveland orchestras. This classification is based partly on the salaries paid to the men, partly on the number of concerts given, and partly on the number of weeks a year the musicians are employed. Take the Boston Symphony: its musicians are employed forty-seven weeks of the year. That is full time, with hardly any leisure beyond their duties to the Boston Symphony for chamber-music concerts, for private teaching, and for teaching in the Conservatory (the New England Conservatory in Boston). This is characteristic of the Class A orchestras. Not only are they Class A in performance, in their abilities, but also in their employment and salary.

Beyond the Class A orchestras there are scores of others, and this is where the greatest development has taken place in the last twenty-five to fifty years, in the enormous numbers of smaller orchestras with seasons much shorter than the metropolitan orchestras. It is a tremendously important field. The United States is, after all, a vast country, and these smaller orchestras in smaller cities and with a shorter history, less financial support, and lower salaries for their players are a very important part of the American orchestra-music picture. Beyond this is another area, the university orchestras. I mentioned before the grandfather of them all, the Pierian Sodality of Harvard, but now there is not an American university or college of importance that does not have its orchestra. Some of them, especially those associated with music schools, or colleges of music, or conservatories within the campus of the university are sometimes very large.

There is another large area in the orchestral-music field, namely the orchestras in the private schools and public high schools. Due to their size, the public high schools are far ahead of most of the private schools in developing orchestras. In the last half-dozen years there have been thirty or more young American composers assigned to high schools, not to teach but to compose and direct music for the high-school orchestras. These appointments, supported by the Ford Foundation, have the title "composer in residence"; I rather dislike that title because I think the composer ought to work in the situation as a *teacher*. After all, Bach was not composer in residence. He was an organist and choirmaster. Palestrina, Mozart, and Haydn were men with duties and a life beyond those of a teacher and different from that of a "composer in residence."

There is one further class of orchestra, that found in music camps, which are summer camps for young people. The largest of these, I suppose, is the famous and quite old music camp at Interlochen, Michigan, where there are several orchestras, a choral department, operatic instructions, and also an intensive program of private lessons. There are many smaller music camps, like the very wonderful Greenwood Music Camp at Cummington, Massachusetts, where as many as a hundred young instrumental players gather together every summer for lessons and for a program of chamber music. Chamber music is a large part of that summer camp, but the orchestra does a concert or two in the course of the season. This is a vast development, ever growing, it seems to me, in the whole picture of orchestral music in the United States.

Perhaps I have omitted one facet, and that is the orchestral development in conservatories. I mentioned music schools associated with universities; but, after all, there are a few American conservatories that go back to the 1860's, like the New England Conservatory in Boston and the Peabody Conservatory in Baltimore. Here too are orchestras, and these conservatory orchestras really provide the recruiting ground for the symphony orchestras of the United States. This is quite a contrast to the earlier days when American players were trained abroad and when the majority of them were European-born. For example, in Boston for forty years most of the players came from Germany; then came the period of Monteux and Koussevitzky, when the players were in large part French musicians who came over to the United States.

MR. PISTON: Here I would like to mention another category, the youth orchestra. This was completely unknown to me until several years ago when I was asked to come to a concert of the Boston Youth Orchestra and I discovered that it had been in existence for some time. The group was playing a new work of mine that I had written for orchestras of a certain professional caliber. I went with fear and trembling, but I must say that I was completely amazed by the professional quality of their performance. The youth orchestra is not connected with any school or any organization like that. It is an orchestra formed for interested young people, who come and practice all season and give concerts. The maximum age for players is about seventeen. This experience was followed by another, even more surprising one.

The California Youth Orchestra wrote and asked whether they could borrow the parts of my Fourth Symphony, which they proposed to practice all winter and then play on a Far East tour. I arranged with my publisher to give them the material and thought no more about it. During the summer I received a program and tape recording from Japan, and I must say listening to that fine performance was an experience, because that symphony is difficult even for the Boston Symphony Orchestra. It seems to me that this is an encouraging sign, not only for future orchestral material but also for future education of young people. But when I see a group play as well as any professionals, I say to myself: "They have no business playing as well as this; they don't have good instruments and they haven't been at it long enough." That is something new and growing all the time.

There is a New York youth symphony orchestra and they play anything. They will perform any piece of modern music because the young are not inhibited by the aura of the masters, although they must have studied the masters or they would not be able to play the way they do. They give really professional programs. Speaking of schools, I visited Dartmouth College as a composer in residence and found the young people there playing all kinds of instrumental groups, from string quartets to even a duo of mine for viola and cello. They also have a fine symphony orchestra composed mainly of students, which is touring the country. Therefore I feel quite encouraged about the future of the symphony orchestra. Another thing that encouraged me at Dartmouth was the audiences; the concerts were completely sold out. Many of the people had never heard a symphony orchestra before, and this development is but a half-dozen years old.

MR. WOODWORTH: There is one point that your remarks have just suggested to me. One hears among serious musicians, critics, and composers the opinion that the latest mode and style of composition in the United States is based mainly upon the Schoenberg-Webern school.

As the result of the cultivation of short pieces, the serial technique and scoring for chamber-music combination, the young American composers are not writing for the orchestra anymore. One even hears orchestral managers worrying about the future of the orchestra, and about its role in modern composition.

I always refer to the "durable symphonic tradition," which began over two hundred years ago with Haydn's First Symphony in 1759. Is that durable tradition finally in 1967 or 1968 or maybe 1970 going to come to an end? What would you say about the position of the American composer in this rather frightening development?

MR. PISTON: The young composers are going through a difficult time and they are trying everything. I urge them always to write what they want to and to push it as far as they can to find out what is in it for them. They naturally react against the gigantic masses of some of the Mahler symphonies and that type of thing.

I do not think that you need to worry about the durability of the literature of music. We have never had so much music; this big mass of music is going to protect itself. It seems to me that the symphony orchestra will probably become a little more flexible—they will not mind if many of them do not play during a

17

whole concert, and one will be able to draw on the orchestra for any kind of combination of instruments. And there will be so many concerts of contemporary music in smaller forms that the symphony orchestra will not need to play them. That, I think, is less hopeless than some try to make out. I know personally that people want to hear music much more than they did when I was young, that is to say, new music. And they are always asking for it.

A flexibility in the symphony orchestra would be helpful in many ways. It would be very beneficial to the orchestra because the single players would be drawn from all the ranks: they would have the responsibility of being soloists in a chamber-music sense; and they would also have the opportunity to get acquainted with the newest music in all forms and would thus increase their musical knowledge as well as their technique. Naturally it would also be a fine thing for the composers because their works could be heard, and heard under the best circumstances.

One of the aspects that come to mind is the relationship of the performer to the composer. I have the old-fashioned notion that the performer is about as important as the composer, and I have an affection for instruments and therefore when I compose music I write it so it can be played. I write it especially to find out for myself what the player thinks of my music. The opposite attitude is one that most people do not know exists among young composers—but I think it has always existed. I once had a young student who brought me, as they often do, a score, and I said to him: "You know this can't be played." His face brightened up. He asked: "Oh, do you really think so?" I replied: "Well, I don't think it can be played." It so happened that I was expecting shortly a certain group of symphony players who were coming to play for a class. The boy copied out the parts laboriously, and after they arrived the performers tried to play it. They started but could not go on; they threw up their hands and said: "We can't play it." It was so complicated with the type of rhythmic variations that one can do easily enough with a computer but not with a human brain. We all looked at the boy and said: "You see, it can't be played." He then exclaimed with great delight: "This is wonderful!"—This kind of approach I find hard to understand. But after a number of experiences like that, I think this boy would come to realize that music after all is written to be played.

The flexible function of the orchestra would also have economic advantages. To prepare a concert of new music would not cost as much as having the symphony members sitting and waiting out the part of the program in which they do not play. More concerts could be given, and the public would have a chance to hear more new music.

MR. WOODWORTH: Looking back over half a century of concert-going, especially symphony concerts, this question comes up: Is the size of the public for orchestra increasing with the new developments in the most recent times?

MR. PISTON: I think there is no doubt at all that both the size of the public and the number of orchestras in the different fields we have mentioned are increasing.

MR. WOODWORTH: I am not a quoter of statistics, but I am sure that the number of concert-goers has increased enormously in Professor Piston's lifetime and in mine. That group of people numbers in the thousands, in the millions; but there are also the listeners to records, to radio, and to television who have multiplied beyond all count—young people and people of all ages. Among the young students whom I know well through my work in the university, nearly every one owns a phonograph; and though they may begin by listening to jazz, possibly rock 'n' roll, soon they go to the record stores to buy recordings of symphonic music.

There are fashions in this field. One thinks, for example, of the tremendous growth of interest in Vivaldi and the Italian concerto composers of the Baroque period; this was unthinkable in my days as a student. This was due to the superb playing of the small Italian string groups that have visited the United States in increasing numbers in recent years. There is a rise and fall, I think, in the stars of different composers. Take Sibelius, for example. Though he always seems to me, because of the Seventh Symphony, a really important figure in symphonic music, fewer records of Sibelius are sold nowadays; and there are fewer performances of Sibelius by most American orchestras than there were twenty-five years ago. In contrast, Bartók's star is constantly rising.

These fashions are found in respect to particular composers, but by and large the sale of records and the listening to good-music stations on radio, plus the sizable number of symphonic performances that are available on television—all these indicate a durable and increasing audience.

MR. PISTON: But one of the sad things is that if one could take soundings now in the 1960's in the United States, it would be discovered that there is a good deal less interest in contemporary music than there was at any other time in history. This worries people like myself who are greatly interested in the fortunes of contemporary composers.

But if we examine the situation of the American symphony orchestra and symphonic literature in general, we see every evidence that the public is getting to know and to like it better. This augurs well for the future of symphony orchestras and for the symphony itself.

MR. WOODWORTH: As you can tell from everything that Professor Piston and I have said, we are optimistic about the symphony orchestra. This has been a kind of survey of the situation in America, and from it I think we can conclude that there is always going to be a public for symphonic music and for music for large orchestra.

We have tried to evaluate the past and have brought the discussion up to the present day, that point at which the future is uncertain. In any historical discussion or survey this is the point at which one has to end.

3 THE BOSTON SYMPHONY ORCHESTRA AND THE BERKSHIRE MUSIC CENTER

Erich Leinsdorf

The Boston Symphony Orchestra, now in its eighty-sixth consecutive year of operation, is a typical American orchestra. I stress this because I have found through the years that the European newspapers and even the more thoughtful and informed among the public still consider symphony orchestras and opera companies in the United States European islands in an otherwise American setup. This is a basic misunderstanding of the American scene. If you look through the roster of the Boston Symphony Orchestra you find: a Norwegian name such as Knudson, a Swedish Madsen, Danish Hansen, Finnish Kahila, Polish Barwicki, Russian Manusevitch, Czech Panenka, Austrian Krips, Hungarian Nagy, Italian Mazzeo, Spanish Valerio, French Voisin, and so on . . . and naturally English names, etc., making a total of seventeen nationalities.

All these men are Americans, and without looking at their birth certificates or their parents' birth certificates, I am unable to tell you if they are immigrants or if their fathers and mothers were immigrants, or if they were born here.

This country is in the best sense of the word a mixture of nationalities. And the cosmopolitanism which these names mark is represented musically by the cosmopolitan style of the Boston Symphony. By cosmopolitan style I mean a style that tries to do

21

artistic justice on the highest level to a wide variety of music. I remember very well from my youth and my years of study in Europe that in our own training very little attention was paid to that repertoire which was not considered "our own." I know that this is the case in many European countries and, as a result, the teaching of instruments, the repertoire study of concert artists is more limited. Here in the United States, particularly in Boston, we not only cultivate an internationally broad repertoire because of public demand and the general taste of our musical public, but we could not exist with a small repertoire, considering that each winter we play a minimum of twenty-four different programs.

This means that at *least* twenty-four entirely different symphony concerts are presented each season. And make no mistake, we do not repeat every year the four Brahms symphonies and the nine Beethoven symphonies. I am particularly careful in my own program policy in Boston to space these great works so as to leave enough room between repeated appearances to keep them fresh for the public as well as for the players and myself. There is nothing more dangerous than to run dry on great works and take them for granted. Taking for granted is the beginning of routine, and routine, as we are all aware, is the death of really inspired performances.

Let me list a few salient statistics about the Boston Symphony. The orchestra works for forty-seven weeks and has a four-week vacation in the summer and one week off at Christmas; parts of the orchestra have rotating vacations, one in the winter and one in the spring. The activities of the orchestra are divided into three major chapters, so to speak. There is the winter season of thirty-one weeks (twenty-four in Boston, five on tour, one exclusively for recordings, and one vacation). Then comes a nine-week season of Pops concerts (Pops is a colloquial abbreviation for Popular), which is a very typically old Bostonian establishment and which gives to the large masses who are not yet willing to face a symphony program the chance to hear waltzes, marches, some of the lighter concerti, and some of the more recently popular show songs and tunes. These concerts take place during the spring after the end of the regular season with an orchestra exactly identical with that in the winter, less a dozen of the first-chair men.

These first-chair men who do not play the Pops concerts form, under the management of the Boston Symphony Corporation, the Boston Symphony Chamber Players. In that combination they give concerts and they play for recordings. This is a very significant and uniquely Boston institution which takes into account the very high individual accomplishments of musicians who desire while being members of an orchestra to retain their artistic identity by playing chamber music. In European orchestras, which are somewhat differently organized, it is not uncommon for the first-violin player and first-cello player to have extended leaves of absence to concertize. This would not be possible in our schedule, but still we recognize that these great individual musicians must be able to operate outside the more choric demands of their orchestral parts.

The third period in the Boston Symphony's operations is the festival at Tanglewood, which is an eight-week summer season. Europeans will readily recognize this as the kind of summer festival that has cropped up all over the Western world during the past three decades, where the traveler, the motorist, the tourist takes his car and his family for the double purpose of having a weekend in a beautiful sylvan setting and listening to great music in a place that is both outdoors and yet protected from the elements of an unfriendly cloudburst. The Tanglewood season is named after the estate which was given to the Boston Symphony some thirty years ago and on which a shed was built (a shed is a structure that has a roof but no sides). A few years ago the acoustics of the shed were greatly improved, so much so that not only can the six thousand people who can be accommodated in the tent hear every note, but people who sit on the lawn outside the shed are also able to hear such delicate things as a violin solo or a light soprano voice.

There is another aspect of Tanglewood which I should mention. This is the Berkshire Music Center, the Boston Symphony's summer center for the advanced study of music. In 1965 the Music Center celebrated its twenty-fifth anniversary. The Berkshire Music Center owes its existence to the vision of Sergey Koussevitzky and to the conscience of the Boston Symphony Orchestra's trustees, who founded the Center in 1940. The Music Center in Tanglewood is a summer academy, not a school. It supplements existing conservatories and music departments at universities, and it is quite clear that in eight weeks one can add decisively to the development of well-schooled musicians but one cannot possibly give them fundamentals.

The trustees, administration, and players of the Boston Symphony and myself are convinced that in giving young musicians the opportunity to attend the Music Center a distinct and unique contribution can be made toward a better balanced musical establishment in the United States and indeed in many countries, as we welcome many from abroad each summer.

To our new Performance Department we admit a maximum of one hundred instrumentalists, singers, and composers. Each of these young musicians is awarded a fellowship stipend enabling him to devote his summer exclusively to his art without monetary pursuit. The program includes all the performance groups on a new postgraduate level, as well as lectures and discussions and an amalgamation of the contemporary music program into the regular course, including the entire expanse of music in every member's studies.

The Tanglewood Institute offers to musical laymen, teachers, and nonperforming musicians a milieu of performances of the highest quality, in addition to a series of specialized seminars. Those who work in the larger field of school and amateur music will find here guidance, stimulation, and new ideas.

The Boston Symphony has a distinguished tradition of serving not only the golden classic, romantic, and contemporary standard works but also of giving first performances of problematic scores as well as the most easily accepted ones. We have at this moment a very significant school of younger composers who are frankly experimenting with new sonorities, some of them with serialism, and just as the better-known older generation of composers, such as Piston, Copland, William Schuman, are represented, so do we take great care to give a proper place in our season's concerts to the avant-garde. This does not mean that we are accepting such joke music as the *Concerto for Piano and Mother,* or things where people drink out of shoes on stage. This headline-catching type of creativity we leave to vaudeville, to night clubs, or to specially arranged festivals. We do, however, have room and time for all serious endeavors in music. Not all of it is kindly accepted by the players or the public, but certainly Boston audiences show (and this again is a very fortunate tradition) great respect for even those things to which they do not take with enthusiasm or even with approval.

We had last year another first—a composer in residence with the Boston Symphony. This is a pilot project (pilot project meaning an experiment which, if successful, will be continued). The Rockefeller Foundation liked the idea and gave the Boston Symphony the necessary special grant to make its realization possible. The idea, which I devised, has as its basis the regrettable fact that many of the younger contemporary composers have turned away from the symphony orchestra as, to them, a sympathetic medium to express their musical ideas. They have chosen instead odd combinations of a few players with much percussion and with voice, but not anything which orchestras with their normal complement of players can do. It seemed to me that during the last few years particularly, less and less effort was made by young composers to write for symphony orchestra; and I felt that part of the cause was not only the length of time necessary to write orchestral scores but, strange to say, their lack of knowledge of the orchestra, particularly significant in a generation that likes to experiment with sonorities.

When you experiment with sonorities, you must have the most intimate knowledge of the medium in which you do your search and your experimentation. And thus I felt that it would be helpful to the composers as well as to the orchestras in the long run to have young composers reside with orchestras, live with them, as it were, for a year, and during that year really get to know what the symphony orchestra can do and how it can do it. We found what I hope is the right man, a composer by the name of John Huggler who had been on the faculty and was a Fellow with a grant at Cornell University, and whose existing scores seemed to me original enough, significant enough, to give him the opportunity of profiting from this year, and of giving the foundation the opportunity through a good pilot to get the necessary cooperation to prove that the theory on which the grant was based was a good one and should be made into a general project in which several of our orchestras can participate.

The present trend of activities of orchestras in the United States is one of covering all aspects in music, of appearing in concerts, on television, of broadcasting on radio, and of making recordings. The Boston Symphony has for I do not know how many years (but it is a very long time) recorded exclusively for RCA Victor, and we produce approximately ten to eleven long-playing records a year. We are now embarked on two cycles: one will encompass all the major works of Prokofiev, and the other, I hope, will after the necessary number of years comprise all the symphonies of Gustav Mahler. We have already recorded Prokofiev's Fifth and Sixth symphonies, the Cello Symphony Concerto, the second version of the Cello Concerto, the First Violin Concerto, and the First, Second, and Fifth piano concerti; and we are planning to continue with the *Romeo and Juliet* music, not the concert suites, but a far more extensive excerpt directly from the ballet score; and more of the several concerti for piano and violin. Of Mahler we have done the First, Fifth, and Sixth symphonies. The Fifth and Sixth symphonies make up three sides of long-playing records, and we had the idea to complete the record on the fourth side with music by Alban Berg. So there is a good possibility that quite without grand design we may put a lot of Berg's music back to back with Mahler, which certainly seems an appropriate enough combination.

I think that the activities of the Boston Symphony give the clearest possible evidence, to anyone who wants this kind of evidence, that American musical life today is as sophisticated as the most exquisite taste can hope for. I find that the Boston organization has the fortunate arrangement that all the commercial music of the more broadly selling variety is done by the Boston Pops, giving to the Boston Symphony a kind of artistic freedom which very few orchestras and very few music directors of orchestras at this moment enjoy any place in the world.

4 THE SAN FRANCISCO SYMPHONY ORCHESTRA: A WESTERN OUTPOST

Josef Krips and Alfred V. Frankenstein

ALFRED V. FRANKENSTEIN: I should like to begin by sketching in very briefly the history and something of the special status of the San Francisco Symphony Orchestra. First of all, I want to point out that the San Francisco Symphony was founded in 1911, and is therefore in its fifty-sixth year. It was founded by Henry K. Hadley, who was rather more interested in composition than in conducting and who left after four years. In its fifty-six years, the San Francisco Symphony has been identified with three outstanding conductors: Alfred Hertz, who was the director from 1915 until 1930; Pierre Monteux, who was the conductor from 1936 until 1952, and Enrique Jordá, who had the orchestra in the late fifties and early sixties. Our present conductor and distinguished participant in the present discussion, Mr. Josef Krips, has been conductor of the San Francisco Symphony for the past four years. He has, in all probability, conducted every major orchestra throughout the Western world.

The San Francisco Symphony occupies a rather special position among American orchestras. This is by no means unique so far as European orchestras are concerned, but it is unique, I believe, in this country in that it is an opera orchestra as well as a concert orchestra. The orchestra plays some two months every fall for the San Francisco Opera Company, which means that the symphony season is delayed in its start until the early part of December. The San Francisco Symphony probably starts its season later than any other major orchestra in America. Yet this circumstance, I suspect, gives the San Francisco Symphony a certain versatility, as it plays both for opera and for symphony concerts, and likewise as an opera orchestra it plays under a great variety of conductors.

Mr. Krips, would you comment on this? Do you find it a true statement of the San Francisco Symphony's position?

JOSEF KRIPS: I think it is true, and it is a really good thing that an orchestra plays both in opera and in symphony concerts. It will play opera better because a symphonic orchestra in general plays better than an opera orchestra. The approach is different. My orchestra members are wonderful readers, which is very important because we have a very limited amount of time to rehearse each program. We have eleven rehearsal hours for each program, during which time we have to prepare one and sometimes two new works in addition to the classic repertoire. For this purpose you need an orchestra that can really read and that can work fast.

Q.: *Do you find the circumstances and conditions of preparing symphony concerts in America very different from what they are in Europe?*

MR. KRIPS: No, I do not think they are.

MR. FRANKENSTEIN: Do you think the orchestras are any different as orchestras?

MR. KRIPS: I would not say so. There are no real basic differences. In Europe there are, of course, great orchestras and lesser orchestras, and the same is true in America. When an orchestra has enough rehearsals and an adequate conductor, it can give good performances. If an orchestra has not enough rehearsal time or has not an adequate conductor, the performances will not be good. The only difference between here and Europe is that in Europe the orchestras are state supported; they are not here. But maybe there was also something good before government support became the rule in Europe.

MR. FRANKENSTEIN: In what respect?

MR. KRIPS: Because no one knew whether he would be engaged the following season, no one could take it easy. From the first day of his engagement until the day of retirement, he had to keep up his ability through practicing. He could never say, after two years of engagement: "Well, now I am sure nothing can happen to me anymore whether I am good or not so good." It was and is entirely different here in America because after twenty years someone could still be called to play an audition. This is not the case in European orchestras. But I still hope that the day will come when the American government will support orchestras in one way or another. The time must come when the American orchestras are employed twelve months, as they are in Europe. And we already have, I think, four orchestras with a fifty-two-week season and even a three-week paid vacation. This is absolutely necessary to keep an orchestra on a high standard and give it security. Up until several years ago most people in the orchestras in smaller towns had to do other things than play music when the winter season was over. They had to work as clerks and in other jobs, and that is not good.

Q.: *I wonder whether I might ask Mr. Krips what his feelings are about the support of the city for the Symphony Orchestra. Are you entirely satisfied with it?*

MR. KRIPS: I must say I was astonished at how good the support is, but we never have enough. I think San Francisco supports it very well, and I am very happy to see that the concerts are well attended, and not only at the concerts and in the Opera House. We twice tried the newly decorated Civic Auditorium, and had a full house with *The Messiah,* and, of course, on Johann Strauss night. You see, it is very necessary that we have possibilities to make money for the orchestra, because it has an enormous budget. In 1964 for the first time the orchestra was paid for the two weeks at Christmastime. So we had to find something that would bring the money—*The Messiah,* with more than six thousand people in the audience, and Johann Strauss, with the same number, made this possible.

MR. FRANKENSTEIN: I am very glad you brought up this point and I think we ought to elaborate on it a bit. One of the distinct and peculiar facts about the San Francisco Symphony is that all of its regular subscription concerts are given three times. Usually American orchestras are satisfied with two performances a week. This orchestra gives three, and performs them in a large hall. The War Memorial Opera House has a seating capacity of thirty-three hundred.

MR. KRIPS: Even a little more.

MR. FRANKENSTEIN: It means roughly that this orchestra plays to ten thousand people a week. Now an even more interesting and distinctive fact about the San Francisco Symphony is that one of its audiences is almost entirely composed of students from the colleges of the Bay region. This started about twenty years ago when some of the college students were invited to establish an organization of their own to fill up the seats here and there. This became so popular and so successful that ultimately an entire series was instituted for the students alone. They take over the entire house every Wednesday night. The orchestra also has a very remarkable series in a place called Foothill College, some thirty miles away from here, in an auditorium that seats twenty-eight hundred.

MR. KRIPS: We never had a concert there which was not sold out. Imagine people sitting on those bleachers. It is unbelievable; last year we went there twelve times.

MR. FRANKENSTEIN: The decentralization of activities is a development in the San Francisco Symphony that I personally have welcomed very much. I would like to see it happen even more. It is part of the whole problem of the American city, and the decentralization of population in American cities with which the orchestras are quite understandably slow to catch up. The population moves out. We build big bridges so people can get out of town fast. We build great freeways for the same purpose and then we are astonished that they do not come back into town for the concerts. The orchestra has to follow the trends of population, and it is finally beginning to do that. The Los Angeles Philharmonic has done it for many years, playing fifty or sixty concerts in its enormous metropolitan area. That is something that I am sure we will come to.

MR. KRIPS: Three years ago we made a beginning in San Mateo.

Q.: *Does the state of California provide any support for its symphony orchestras?*

MR. KRIPS: I could not say.

MR. FRANKENSTEIN: No, not that I am aware of. The city of San Francisco provides a certain amount of support for this orchestra. I would like to discuss that a bit, because it created a very difficult situation. When I first came here, more than thirty years ago, the San Francisco Symphony, in the backwash of the great depression of 1929, was in a very bad way financially; so the city passed a charter amendment whereby a certain percentage of the taxes was automatically given to the Symphony Orchestra. But this created a bad situation, because the orchestra then had to give a series of concerts under the auspices of the city that was in competition with its regular subscription series. This resulted in a very difficult and curious state of affairs that was finally resolved by the orchestra's playing for the city in the summer, doing a series of Pops concerts. It has been said, by the way, that the orchestra earns 37 per cent more from its regular series than any other orchestra in this country.

Q.: *I realize I was asking a rather difficult question there. Mr. Frankenstein, how do you conceive of the function of the critic vis-à-vis the symphony orchestra?*

MR. FRANKENSTEIN: Let me say that one of the functions of a critic is perennially to point out the orchestra's deficiencies and the way in which it falls short of its ideal in order that, perhaps, the orchestra might be kept a little on its toes. This, of course, is only part of it. Another part is obviously "the noble art of praising." In fact, the noble art of praising is one which, under Mr. Krips, we have been able to indulge in with increasing frequency and which I am quite sure we shall continue to indulge in.

Q.: *Mr. Krips, may I ask how you see the function of criticism?*
MR. KRIPS: Well, I think criticism is very necessary despite the fact that what the critic says is his opinion and must not always be the opinion of others. But as long as a critic is objective, as long as he criticizes and says "I did not like the program because of this," I accept it. Many times I learn from it. I think criticism will always be a healthy thing.

MR. FRANKENSTEIN: I think one of the most amusing and entertaining hours I have ever spent in my life was in Sacher's Restaurant in Vienna, when Mr. Krips was host at dinner, after a magnificent performance of *Der Rosenkavalier* at the Opera House across the street, to two critics bearing the same fantastic name of Alfred Frankenstein, two totally different people of totally different backgrounds and ancestries both serving as music critics in two totally different parts of the world. I, who have lived most of my life in San Francisco, and my friend and colleague, Alfred Frankenstein, who has lived most of his life in Tel Aviv and who writes for Hebrew- and German-language papers in Israel, met for the first time in our lives as guests of Mr. Krips in Sacher's Restaurant eating enormous quantities of *Sal—*

MR. KRIPS: *Salzburger Nockerln.*

Q.: *How was the encounter between the two critics?*
MR. FRANKENSTEIN: We had a lot of fun.

MR. KRIPS: It was very fascinating, because one of them is really very advanced. That is our Alfred Frankenstein in San Francisco, who favors contemporary music, sometimes even more than I would like; Mr. Frankenstein from Tel Aviv hates any kind of contemporary music, and so it was a wonderful discussion. Even when the name of Prokofiev came up, Frankenstein from Tel Aviv said: "My God, these contemporary composers! Isn't it terrible, as long as we have Mozart and Haydn?" So we had a discussion about all kinds of avant-garde music. You see, it is absolutely the task of a symphony orchestra to bring the repertoire up to date. I say that as long as something is music, I perform it. But there are some composers, or whatever you want to call them, who no longer make music; they just make sounds or noises. If someone buys a ticket to hear a symphony concert, he wants to hear a symphony orchestra. And there are enough good contemporary composers who can be performed. We have something new in every program. We have had the first performance of a composer named Kirk Mechum, really a remarkable piece. The young man is able to write a symphony (especially the last movement). It is really heart-warming. We did "Kaddish" by Bernstein which is perhaps one of the most difficult pieces I have conducted in my life. It is more difficult than any Stravinsky. We had a performance of a work by Darius Milhaud, *Pacem in Terris*. We do what we can, considering the short rehearsal time we have for preparing new works; sometimes I have to conduct from a manuscript score that is hardly readable.

Q.: *Do you find that your audiences in San Francisco take readily to the modern composers that you introduce to them?*

MR. KRIPS: They react wonderfully, I think. They react wonderfully even when I do not expect it.

MR. FRANKENSTEIN: It seems to me as an observer from the audience's side that the Wednesday-night audience, that unique group of young people, is particularly receptive. One would expect it to be, but to actually experience it is something else again. It is a wonderfully warm and responsive kind of audience to play to.

MR. KRIPS: But, imagine, the Mechum symphony made an enormous success, even Thursday afternoon with our ladies from the Bay area. It was unbelievable. Also "Kaddish." And I get many letters; the Friday audience is not bad at all. I cannot complain about the public. There is real interest. Also outside San Francisco in Foothill College, you can give, let me say, a program of Alexei Haieff's Second Symphony and Boardman's First Symphony, both played for the first time, both in the same concert. That is something.

MR. FRANKENSTEIN: You spoke a moment ago of limitations of time in preparing a work like Bernstein's "Kaddish." Would you find less limitations in preparing a work like that, say in Vienna?

MR. KRIPS: I am sure we would have a little more time.

MR. FRANKENSTEIN: Significantly enough time?

Q.: *May I ask why?*

MR. KRIPS: Because we have a certain number of services. We have eight services, and the services have to be four rehearsals and four concerts. When we need more time we have to pay extra, and that is quite a sum of money. I imagine when you have a work where you have to pay the chorus (we now use the opera chorus) and you have a soloist or a narrator, it comes to quite a bit of money. We had extra instruments for the "Kaddish," and so we had four hours of rehearsal. The orchestra works very fast.

Q.: *I wonder if I might ask about the facilities in which you perform, about the hall that San Francisco has for its Symphony Orchestra concerts?*

MR. KRIPS: I think we should be very happy with what we have. The Opera House is a wonderful building, and since we have the new shell made by Heinrich Keilholtz, I think we should be satisfied. It took time for us to adjust. We no longer play on risers. The whole orchestra sits flat on the floor under the shell. I think the acoustics are now very satisfactory. Nowadays it is very difficult with new halls, because most of them are a disappointment, except for one hall that I think is just marvelous, the Montreal Hall. It is wonderful. I do not know the new hall in Los Angeles.

MR. FRANKENSTEIN: I have heard concerts in the new hall in Los

35

Angeles and I find it very good. Indeed, the fact that Los Angeles got a brand-new, very fine, handsome, acoustically excellent concert hall caused a considerable repercussion in San Francisco. A new hall also went up in San Diego, a large and acoustically quite good one, and this again created a certain repercussion in San Francisco because the San Francisco Opera House is over thirty-five years old and did require some acoustical rearrangements.

Q.: *It might be interesting to discuss any acoustical problems you might have had that led to the development of the shell you now have.*

MR. FRANKENSTEIN: Bear in mind, first of all, that the hall where the San Francisco Symphony plays is actually an opera house. It was built for opera. It has a large pit, and it has a very deep and very large stage, and it is used quite extensively for opera. As such, it is now obsolete and inadequate. So the late president of the San Francisco Symphony, Mr. J. D. Zellerbach, conceived the idea of bringing Mr. Keilholtz here to improve it as much as he could.

MR. FRANKENSTEIN: He promptly did so by providing a very large shell, but at the same time this created certain problems. I am convinced and have repeatedly said that a hall is a musical instrument and that you cannot learn to play a hall the first time, any more than you can play a flute, a cello, or a violin the first time you pick it up. It requires experience. It requires all kinds of experiment. It requires reseating, and so on, which Mr. Krips has done, and he has finally achieved a very satisfactory balance.

Q.: *Have you found any peculiar problems with the seating in that connection?*

MR. KRIPS: We tried different ways of seating. Every orchestra has different seating plans. The Vienna Philharmonic has an entirely different seating than the Concertgebouw. It all depends on the hall where an orchestra is playing. You have to adjust to the acoustical condition. As we have it here, the seating is most satisfactory. First of all, it is no longer possible for the brass or percussion to drown out the rest of the orchestra. My first rule is no fortissimo should be so loud that you cannot hear the violins playing. I think we have achieved a great deal in balance in this orchestra. I must say I am perfectly happy with the hall, and I could not have even conceived of the possibility that we would have something as adequate. Besides that, this opera house is already what I would call a tradition. People like Alfred Hertz, Monteux, and Jordá worked here for years and years. There is something here you know, something that sounds very European, because in Europe we are very proud of everything with tradition. The feeling of every single musician in San Francisco is very strong.

MR. FRANKENSTEIN: Along this line I would like to add that a number of years ago Mr. Leo Beranek, who was the acoustical consultant in the building of Lincoln Center, came to San Francisco. I had a very long discussion with him. One of the things we agreed upon was that you could not build into Lincoln Center some forty or fifty years of use, and the nice ghosts which go with it.

Q.: *The drama of past concerts?*

MR. FRANKENSTEIN: Yes, I mean, after all, what can you do in a hall where Toscanini has been conductor for many years? There is something there. I'm quite sure Mr. Krips is correct in saying that there has been a very good tradition in the hall, not only with the symphony but with the opera as well.

Q.: *Some of the leading performing artists have been full of praise in speaking of the talents of American symphony orchestras vis-à-vis those in Europe. Mr. Krips, would you make a few observations on the relationship of the conductor and the performer? Who, for example, selects the concerto to be played?*

MR. KRIPS: The conductor makes the program. I complete the programs for the coming season by the end of January. Then I go to the president and say that I want these and these soloists and submit the programs. Up to now the management has been very happy with the programs and soloists I submitted. Also, the program that the soloist plays is made by me. That is the procedure.

MR. FRANKENSTEIN: How do you work out the conception of the work? Do you generally defer to the artist in his conception of the work to be done?

MR. KRIPS: Usually when I need a soloist for a Mozart concerto I know whom I want, and when I want a contemporary concert I know exactly whom to ask. We have many young talents in the Bay area, too, and I try to hear all of them. I recently had about eight or ten pianists and some violin players and all kinds of others play for me. I think there is a lot of talent, and if a soloist comes from outside he must be an outstanding man; otherwise I try to put in a local person. After the last season came to an end, we did a Beethoven festival with all nine symphonies and piano concertos, the triple concerto, and the violin concerto; I used mostly soloists from the West Coast. This was the only regular subscription season without the name of Beethoven on it. There were twenty concerts. When we did the whole Beethoven festival —the Beethoven cycle—we did it this way, and maybe one day we will do the same with Brahms or Bruckner or Berlioz. There are many possibilities.

MR. FRANKENSTEIN: It has been done here before, in Monteux's time, particularly the Brahms cycle and the Beethoven cycle. The public particularly likes the idea of a cycle. You can play all nine Beethoven symphonies and scatter them through the whole season, but it does not seem to add up the same way as when you play them in immediate succession. I used to see this in the record programs I did on the radio. I could play all the Beethoven symphonies in the course of a month and never announce it was a Beethoven cycle. They would like it all right. But if I announced that we were going to present a Beethoven cycle, devoting one program a week to Beethoven symphonies and concertos, the public response was always much stronger.

MR. KRIPS: In London, when I was conductor in chief of the London Symphony Orchestra, we had a Beethoven cycle each year for ten years in succession. It did the orchestra a lot of good in every respect.

MR. FRANKENSTEIN: About twenty-five years ago, a chapter of the International Society for Contemporary Music was formed in the Bay region. I am not putting it quite properly. What actually happened was that a group of the Bay Region composers got together, formed an organization, and applied to the International Society for Contemporary Music for a charter as a chapter. They received back from the London headquarters of the society the suggestion that they join the Tokyo branch inasmuch as Tokyo was closer to San Francisco than London. This is a peculiarly London point of view toward San Francisco, but as has been pointed out, we are much closer, actually, to the Orient than we are to Europe. This creates a rather special situation with regard to the San Francisco Symphony. Among other things, it means that the rival and foreign orchestras that could come through and help to keep the orchestra a little more on its toes come through rather seldom. The Philadelphia Orchestra has come through occasionally, the Boston Symphony once or twice. Last season the Chicago Symphony came, and the London Symphony has also been here.

MR. KRIPS: The Cleveland Orchestra also appeared.

MR. FRANKENSTEIN: But it is still a rare and exceptional experience for an Eastern, and particularly for a European, orchestra to come here. We do not have a similar situation to that in New York, where the Philadelphia Orchestra and the Boston Symphony play a regular season, and so on. This also means, however, that the San Francisco Symphony players are spread out in more directions than commonly. We have already mentioned the fact that this is an opera orchestra as well as a symphony orchestra. Mr. Krips has mentioned something I neglected to and should have. We have a most interesting spring opera season, with a slightly different repertoire and a younger group of singers. Our orchestra plays for them. We also have a very interesting ballet company in San Francisco for which the orchestra plays a great deal. Then we have a series of youth concerts with the symphony (about fourteen a season) which are played all over the area; also the members of the orchestra are constantly splitting off into chamber groups: chamber orchestras and string quartets. There are, if I am not mistaken, two woodwind ensembles composed of the members of the San Francisco Symphony, and so on. As Mr. Krips has observed, a symphony-orchestra musician who does not play chamber music is likely to be a deteriorating symphony-orchestra musician. So it is a good thing. But also what I am trying to say, partly, is that this particular nucleus of orchestral musicians has rather more to do in San Francisco than it would have elsewhere, partly because of the peculiar geographical situation. One thing that might have been expected but is not true is that there is relatively little direct contact with or influence from the musicians of the Orient here and elsewhere in the United States.

Q.: *Over all, however, the San Francisco Symphony presents a rather encouraging picture of the role of the symphony orchestra in the life of the community, does it not?*

MR. KRIPS: I have the feeling that we are on the way if the support remains the same; I do not think that we have to worry too much. Of course, there will always be lots of work to do. Every year come new works we have to perform, and we still have to work on the quality of the orchestra because there is never an end. But, on the whole, the picture does not seem bad.

MR. FRANKENSTEIN: There is a common impression and much discussion of the fact that there is a shortage of good string players in this country. Do you find this true?

MR. KRIPS: After my experience in San Francisco, I cannot say that.

MR. FRANKENSTEIN: That is very interesting, because there have been so many complaints about that. The explanation frequently given is that the young people want to play wind instruments because there is more money to be made immediately with them.

MR. KRIPS: A string instrument, in reality, takes much longer to learn than a wind instrument. But still, let me say, not long ago I was short a viola player, but I would not engage someone just to fill the post. A new player who comes in has to be at least 100 per cent better than the man he is replacing. That is the rule.

Q.: *What was your instrument before you became a conductor?*

MR. KRIPS: Piano, and also violin.

MR. FRANKENSTEIN: Were you playing in the orchestra in Vienna?

MR. KRIPS: I played in an orchestra in Vienna when I was very, very young. In the People's Opera.

MR. FRANKENSTEIN: Played violin?

MR. KRIPS: Yes, for three years, but I haven't touched a fiddle since then. A conductor has to have some experience in the orchestra to know how to deal with orchestra musicians. You see, orchestra musicians are a breed unto themselves. An orchestra musician when he wakes up in the morning is already offended, because he knows beforehand that he will be abused by the conductor, by the management, by the board, by the press, by everybody. So one needs a certain psychological knowledge to deal with these people. But in the end, much good is in them. Don't forget, it is in reality a kind of tragic occupation. Imagine, there are some really very fine musicians. Maybe they have their own opinion about how a piece should be played, yet during their whole career they can do only what others ask them to do. So there is a certain greatness required; it is a very difficult thing. I imagine that every piece is different with each different conductor. I remember once while I was in Vienna, the Vienna Philharmonic had two tours. One was going to London and Paris and was very short, and it was conducted by Felix Weingartner, my former teacher; the other was going to Budapest and Bucharest and was conducted by Bruno Walter. Both had the great C Major Schubert on the program. In the morning Weingartner had a three-hour rehearsal of the C Major Schubert, and in the afternoon Walter had a three-hour rehearsal of the same work. Each did it entirely differently. So it is not always easy to play in an orchestra. The orchestra sounds different under the baton of each different conductor. That is so especially for orchestras which have to deal with many conductors. It is very difficult and always takes a certain amount of time before an orchestra and conductor can become one instrument. I think of the conductor as a member of the orchestra; he has to feel like one. He may be a very important member, but if he does not feel like a member of the orchestra, he never can come near the hearts of his musicians. So those are our problems.

5 THE UTAH SYMPHONY ORCHESTRA: AN ORCHESTRA IN THE DEEP INTERIOR

Maurice Abravanel

Q.: *Mr. Abravanel, how long have you been in Salt Lake City?*
MAURICE ABRAVANEL: I came to Salt Lake City in 1947.

Q.: *Are there any special features in the cultural life of Salt Lake City that you found when you came, or have developed since you came, that you think will help to explain the status of your orchestra?*

MR. ABRAVANEL: Salt Lake City and Utah were settled by Mormon pioneers. They had a musical tradition. Times were hard and on their long journey from the East, which took them many months, the Mormons used to sing together at night. When they arrived in this valley, they had only the bare necessities of life. But the first thing they built was a hall where they could sing and dance. This is the only place I know of in the United States where people came, not in pursuit of a materially better life but because of an idea. That naturally gives a certain color to the Utah population, whether Mormon or not. Choral singing is an old Mormon tradition; they sing a great deal in their churches and at home. Therefore there is a rich choral background in Utah.

Q.: *When you came, did you find very much in the way of instrumental music?*

MR. ABRAVANEL: No, instrumental music was relatively undevel-

43

oped. When the pioneers made their long journey across the plains, they carried a violin with them. They had a few musicians among them, and from the beginning they tried to have orchestras.

Q.: *What sort of musical interest did you find in the field of instrumental music? In other words, what kind of classical music did the citizens know when you came?*

MR. ABRAVANEL: Well, it was very amusing. When this orchestra became interested in engaging me, I was on the way to San Francisco to conduct. I stopped at Salt Lake City and asked for the programs; I found that the *Eroica,* the Ninth Symphony, the *Jupiter,* Brahms's Second, and Schubert's C Major had never been played. I told them if they would engage me, I would naturally play those works. They warned me that the people there were not sophisticated and probably would not take it. So I told them that inasmuch as it costs money anyhow to run a symphony orchestra, let us spend what we have on the best and see what happens.

Q.: *A fascinating development, then, has taken place in the time you have been here, hasn't it?*

MR. ABRAVANEL: Well, it is a marvelous thing for a conductor. I cannot think of a greater experience than to go to a concert and feel that now, tonight, people are going to hear the Ninth Symphony for the first time.

Q.: *Please start from the beginning and tell us how this came about.*

MR. ABRAVANEL: I auditioned people with the idea of really making the orchestra a symphony orchestra. I do not believe it is worth having an orchestra in a community made up of people who come the day before the first rehearsal and leave the night of the last concert. I did engage a few musicians for the first year and they stayed two years with me. I engaged outstanding key men. I would audition people, listen to them, and again and again engage people who had never played in an orchestra. In

44

the first rehearsal we barely got through the first movement of the *Eroica*. Many of the musicians occasionally remind me of that event because a number of the same men are still in the orchestra. However, I did engage people who became very good. My musicians are local people, only a few top key men came from the outside, mostly from New York.

Q.: *What in particular have you done to keep musicians from season to season?*

MR. ABRAVANEL: First, I tried to make each happy, and I also remembered that no matter who he is or where he plays a musician is a human being who at some time decided that music was what interested him most in life. I don't think that anybody ever started on that arduous path of music making because he thought it was an easy way to earn a living. I even reminded the New York Philharmonic musicians at a rehearsal: "Look, unless you try to enjoy every minute of your music making, you are really fools. You are all intelligent people, and you could do much better selling herbs or doing anything else in the business line. So, our first duty is to try to work." I am extremely patient as long as I feel a musician is doing his best. All my life I have tried to appeal to this element in the musician—never to make him feel he is a machine.

Q.: *How do you characterize your orchestra? How good is it in your estimation, realizing, of course, that you have an enormous affection for something on which you have lavished so much care during the past twenty years?*

MR. ABRAVANEL: I think I am very objective about this orchestra. Many people say it is much better than many orchestras in cities five times the size. Actually, the orchestra is not better, but it plays better quite often. It has a fantastic *esprit de corps,* a great pride in its work. We have quite a few top musicians who could sit in any orchestra anywhere in the world. My musicians are happy. I have many housewives, students, and young people. My practice when we play a new work at the first rehearsal is to not go too much into detail. They take the parts home and practice.

The quality of this orchestra is a very strange thing; I am not sure how long it can last. When I came, the orchestra's quality was below many other orchestras. Eight services meant early rehearsals every morning and then concerts in the evening. The salaries were very low, so, naturally, people left. No good people will stay for a salary of two or three thousand dollars a year, particularly if they have to raise a family. So I switched to evening rehearsals from six to eight thirty. With rehearsals starting at six o'clock, the musicians can have full-time day jobs, gulp a dinner, and rush to the rehearsal. If they have a band job, they can leave and still rehearse with the band afterward. It is a shoestring, tight-wire, high-rope operation, but it works.

Q.: *Your orchestra sounds very much to me like what the modern educators would call a group of overachievers. Your description of the orchestra tallies with what Martin Mayer, music critic for* Esquire *magazine, has written as an appraisal of the Utah Symphony: "To this orchestra clearly every performance is an occasion, not just a job. The sum becomes much bigger than its parts—which is, after all, what ensemble playing is supposed to produce. The reason why world-renowned soloists try to sneak afternoons off to play a little chamber music. Out of this spirit," he says, "and affection, the Utah Symphony has made itself a major orchestra, far superior to the orchestras of cities four and five times the size and wealth of Salt Lake. One wonders whether its audiences, who know their orchestra as a more or less routine local fixture in the cultural scene, can appreciate how remarkable an achievement they hear on the nights when they 'go to the Symphony.' " I think this is a very beautiful characterization of your orchestra. But it is also a description of the community. We might well turn to some of the spirit and affection that come out of the community for this orchestra. Could you tell us something about the community support for the Utah Symphony Orchestra?*

MR. ABRAVANEL: The community is very proud of its orchestra. I get fan letters all the time; after seventeen years, I still get calls. People stop me on the street and say: "Mozart was so beautiful last night. Can't you record it?" That is the spirit here. You realize we have 3,750 season ticket subscribers for the 13 concert series. The prices, I think, go to $42. The music-going public thus is 2.2 per cent of the total population. As far as contributions are concerned, they are good too, compared to the size of the city. It is the only city this size that has an orchestra that gives some 75 concerts in a season and that records extensively. We now have more than 30 recordings in the catalog. Yet, compared with the quality of the orchestra and the amount of work it does, the contributions are small.

Q.: *How do you budget? How much comes in from the gate, from the ticket sales?*

MR. ABRAVANEL: Our budget now runs to over $500,000. We earn almost 80 per cent of our budget from ticket sales and program advertising, which is three times the amount that is earned by most orchestras. I think the Mormon background has something to do with it. In Mormon country, the day is much longer than anywhere else on earth; Mormons are very industrious. This also affects the lives of non-Mormons. I used to get up very late before coming to Salt Lake City. Now I get up at 5:30 A.M.

Q.: *What do you do to give your musicians more security?*

MR. ABRAVANEL: If somebody plans to get married or wants to buy a house and feels he would like more security, we often give him a three-year contract. I have never fired anybody from the orchestra. If somebody lets down a little, I call him on the phone and draw it to his attention. Usually this yields results. Once in a while the whole orchestra get terribly tired. Then I lecture them a little bit and they see the point. They are happy in their work, and that is all I can say.

Q.: *What do you do to interest young players?*

MR. ABRAVANEL: I started something during my first year with the orchestra. I realized parents will spend money for piano lessons because their child might become another Rubinstein. Violin is more difficult; there are fewer Heifetzes. When it comes to bassoon, bass tuba, etc., who wants to pay anything for instruction? So I instituted a program of developing the most talented young people. First I would hold auditions; anybody who wants may audition. To the really talented ones I would give scholarships with our key people, so that they would have one weekly lesson. For the last twelve years (this will be my thirteenth year) I have been director of the Music Academy of the West in Santa Barbara. There we have some of the best teachers in the country, so I give the best students an opportunity to come to Santa Barbara, many of them on scholarships.

Q.: *Would you tell us a little about Santa Barbara?*

MR. ABRAVANEL: The people there have decided to spend money so that very young people can learn about music, young people on the threshold of professional life.

Q.: *Do they get scholarships there?*

MR. ABRAVANEL: Yes, all those who need scholarships get them.

Q.: *Could you give us a description of how a musician might get started in Salt Lake, and might grow and might end up in your orchestra; also how he would be started privately in the schools and then how his career would develop under this scheme that seems to have developed in Salt Lake City?*

MR. ABRAVANEL: Utah always had a marvelous choral tradition, but whatever instrumental tradition there might have been before was killed when sound movies came in. When the Utah Symphony was started, I needed overnight some sixty, seventy, or eighty players, so a lot of those people had an incentive to work. Today any youngster in Utah who is musically inclined has only one dream: "If I work very hard, someday I might play in the Utah Symphony." We make it a practice to play in any little town that can pay our touring fee, which is, roughly, sixteen hundred dollars. This fee covers only about half our actual cost, but we go—no matter how far. We go yearly to places that have no more than four or five thousand inhabitants. Sometimes it is started by one music teacher or one lady or one weekly newspaper.

In one case our manager got a phone call. A high-pitched voice on the other end asked if they could engage the Utah Symphony and what it would take to bring it there. The manager gave the information and said: "What is your name, madam?" The voice replied: "Bill Horsley." He was a young boy, a junior-high-school-student president with his voice still unchanged. He had decided he wanted the Utah Symphony to come. We agreed to go there for an evening concert. The boy convinced his teachers and principal and they helped sell tickets. When we arrived they were adding extra chairs in that twelve-hundred-seat auditorium in a town of ten thousand.

Q.: *Incredible. While we are considering the life of the musician, I wonder how well the Salt Lake City musician lives. Obviously he is a very busy man, but does he live reasonably well?*

MR. ABRAVANEL: Many of them live much better than their counterparts in most American or European cities, but, of course, at the price of hard work. The first prerequisite to being a member of the Utah Symphony is stamina. I told my players some time ago: "Look, I am going to work toward the goal of a full-time orchestra." Those people were in their twenties, thirties, or forties. "You won't always be able to have your full-time jobs and then come in the evening and play in the Symphony as well as you do," I told them. Well, there was an outcry. They said: "No, we like it the way it is." Now, to talk about the matter realistically, what it means is this: thirty-five of them are music teachers in the school system, so they get their school salary. On top of that, they get their salary in the Utah Symphony. For thirty-five players, in addition to our regular season which is twenty-four weeks plus two weeks where we make recordings, there are easily another fourteen weeks of playing. We have a musical in the fall; we have ballet in the fall; then we have a modern-dance week, a ballet week, and an opera after the season. We have a summer festival under the stars. So about fifty-five of the musicians actually have thirty weeks; thirty-five of them have almost forty weeks. Even with small salaries, if you add that to their daytime salary, they are doing well. It is a crazy situation. These people, on the one hand, are tired physically when they come to our concerts. On the other hand, mentally, emotionally, they are fresh because this is the climax of their day.

Q.: *Not too long ago you did a very large symphony, Symphony Number 8 by Gustav Mahler called* Symphony of a Thousand. *How could you do it?*

MR. ABRAVANEL: It is very simple. I have the young people whom I take to Santa Barbara—a reservoir of players. There are seventy-five musicians under contract for the full season, but I have contracts for extra players, which means those people know that whenever five or six horns are required, or a fourth or fifth trumpet, they are always available. Of course, Mahler takes an enormous orchestra. I have the extra brasses; they were all there, not regular members of the Symphony, but according to the reviews they shine very much on the recordings.

Q.: *How did you do Darius Milhaud's* Pacem in Terris?

MR. ABRAVANEL: *Pacem* was more difficult because the choral singing is very difficult. The orchestra is no problem, but on the chorals I must admit we had great difficulties. It is very hard music to sing and many of those people left. So finally I ended up by calling the Cathedral Choir of St. Mark's and getting all kinds of singers. But Milhaud was very happy.

Q.: *What about your instrumental soloists, I mean, guest soloists?*

MR. ABRAVANEL: The first duty of an orchestra is to stay alive. In order to stay alive in a small city we must be sure a lot of people come to the concerts. The Tabernacle is a very big place,

I discovered. It took me that long to learn that fact. Our greatest contributor was Artur Rubinstein. Even if his fee was very high, the Tabernacle was packed to the rafters when he played. I was rather unhappy about this, but I cannot afford to bring unknown soloists. Each year I have a "Salute to Youth" concert. I audition young people from our state and the best ones play at an evening concert with the Utah Symphony. This is a terrific incentive for the young people.

Q.: *You say the first function of an orchestra is to stay alive. It is quite obvious your orchestra has stayed alive with a great deal of enthusiasm and* esprit. *How does one account for so much* esprit? *Is it the fact that your musicians participate in such magnificent works which many symphony musicians do not have such an opportunity to participate in? Is it the fact that this community is so very much alive? Is it the surroundings? How do you account for these things, Mr. Abravanel?*

MR. ABRAVANEL: As I said before, when I came to Salt Lake City, the *Eroica* and the Ninth Symphony had never been played there. I was told: "We don't think we are sophisticated enough to take these works." I said: "Well, those musicians don't forget my first concert when we played the *Eroica.*" When we played Strauss's *Don Juan,* etc., we were playing them for the first time and they felt the audience was listening to them for the first time. So we were fighting for the life of the *Eroica*—not giving the six thousandth performance where the audience might judge whether this is clear or this is faster or slower or more reliable or more in depth. We were simply fighting to prove that Beethoven was a great man. So it was give and take. The audience felt very proud they could hear those works and enjoy them. Little by little their appreciation was expanded.

By now we have an audience which is absolutely marvelous. When we played the Mahler Eighth, you could have heard a pin drop from beginning to end. They were completely engrossed, and to a foreign musician who sees the audience it makes a big difference whether you play the St. Matthew Passion and you see people with tears running down their cheeks or you see an audience looking at their watches or shuffling their feet. There must be a complete unanimity between musicians and audience. Utahans, don't forget, came here to escape the world; and for one hundred years they did not want the world to know about Utah; so I never knew anything about it. Nothing! I discovered that in Salt Lake you have something you do not even have in Zurich, Switzerland, or Munich. Within forty minutes you have your choice of seven canyons and two or three places where you are at 12,000 feet. We have the best ski slopes. When you go there you find complete silence, which is the rarest commodity today. Complete silence of blue sky, and in the winter, fresh, clean air. I believe these contribute to the atmosphere for making good music.

Q.: *This is a fascinating picture of a musical family which obviously has drawn a great deal of inspiration from you and also from the audience which quite obviously supports it to the extent that 80 per cent of the funds comes from subscriptions. I wonder if I might come back to a more mundane subject, since any good family has to have housekeeping expenses, to the question of where you get the other 20 per cent of your budget for the orchestra?*

MR. ABRAVANEL: We receive a small contribution, which amounts to 3½ per cent of our budget from the state, and a little contribution from the city and the same from the county. We have about three hundred contributors: firms or private individuals who give mostly smaller amounts, very few large amounts. Altogether that makes up the 20 per cent. We give an enormous number of concerts. We travel quite far. We travel up to Boise and down to Las Vegas, into Wyoming, into Colorado, and the only limitation is those daytime shows. We have been asked many times to do touring, which we cannot afford because the musicians cannot leave their jobs for very long.

Q.: *Do you think you get enough subsidy?*

MR. ABRAVANEL: Well, you know the answer to that. Nobody thinks he gets enough. Personally, I am convinced that music, more than any other art, is not only important as an art. We all agree that civilizations and societies are being judged more by their artistic achievements than by anything else, and those naturally include painting, poetry, and sculpture. But I believe music has a completely different function in our modern civilization. On the Lower East Side of New York and in Manhattan they have a music project. For some forty years there have been about forty thousand students enrolled. Not one has ever been hauled to a juvenile delinquency court. I believe very deeply that music is much more than just something for music lovers. I love those boys' clubs and athletic leagues and sandlot leagues and the rest. They are all fine. But when the youngsters come from a basketball or football game, they break windows, steal into cars, and all of that. It is very good for their physical health. It is certainly not good enough for their character because we have more athletes than any other country on earth and many delinquents. But what happens when the youngsters come out of a concert? Seven thousand come to my concerts in the Tabernacle. They leave all excited. And you do not need a single policeman to look after them. So I believe the states and municipalities would save considerably by spending money on music, on good music for children to learn and to play.

Q.: *Is the Tabernacle made available for your concerts?*

MR. ABRAVANEL: The president of the Mormon Church made the best speech for the Utah Symphony many years ago when he said he was very grateful every time we were playing and were on broadcasts because of the good influence. For quite a few years we have been using the Tabernacle for concerts, completely free, which is naturally a very important contribution.

The acoustics are world famous, exceedingly alive and sometimes a little upsetting when the hall is empty. When the hall

53

is full, the sound is marvelous. It enters psychologically, not scientifically, into the field of acoustics. Acoustics are not what your ear gets but what your soul gets. When you sit on those benches in this church building with the beautiful organ in front of you and those big pipes, to me this is a better setting to listen to a Beethoven symphony or a Bach passion or a Mahler piece than many concert halls.

Q.: *How does the fact that you do perform in the Tabernacle affect your programing? Why did you do* Pacem in Terris, *for instance?*

MR. ABRAVANEL: *Pacem in Terris* was first performed on Christmas 1963 in Paris. It was commissioned by the French television for their new radio and television building. I was in Europe on a vacation when I read the message of Pope John XXIII, and to me, this is one of the most important documents of the century, a marvelous document. I did not know that Darius Milhaud took excerpts from it and composed the symphony on it. But I got the piano vocal score the minute it was printed. I saw it and I was fascinated. I took the score and put it in with scores of Darius Milhaud and then forgot it. But it kept coming back to me. I would look for some score and by mistake that would come into my hands. It was one of these rare times that I felt that it is a pity I don't have a choir or audience to perform a work like that. I was so fascinated by it, I finally decided to do it. Naturally the idea of playing in the Mormon Tabernacle a work in Latin, written by a great contemporary composer, appealed to me tremendously. Darius Milhaud came for the performance and got an ovation that lasted four minutes. Personally, I love all kinds of music, but I have always liked the great works. I have always wanted to do these works more than the little things. The Tabernacle helps.

Q.: *What is your idea of programing?*

MR. ABRAVANEL: In Salt Lake City the orchestra is only nineteen years old. Everybody wants to hear the great works again and again. They are not yet familiar with them. I never play a work more than once in three or four or five years—even Beethoven's Fifth. So when I play it again, it is brand-new. I conduct the standard works, the ones I think are important. I give a lot of American works and many works by Utah composers. We did a Mass by Scarlatti, the first American performance. We did the first American recording of *King David* (*Le Roi David*) and of *Judith* by Honegger.

Q.: *Do you have complete freedom to make up your programs?*

Mr. Abravanel: I have complete freedom in program-making, the choice of soloists (subject to their fees being agreeable to management), about personnel matters, and more than that, about the number of concerts and rehearsals. I work very fast. I have to. But if I feel the need of one more rehearsal, I do not have to ask anybody. I just rehearse.

I went through a very bad experience the second year I was in Salt Lake City. The money ran out and the board decided to fold in the middle of the season. We could not go on because there was no money left. I kept the orchestra together, telling them that if those who could afford to come in, could, and if I had thirty-two musicians, I would play. So we went on playing. Since that day I have been watching the budget very closely. We are thrifty and careful. I know that anything is better than going through that experience again of having to phone nice people to say: "Unless you come through we have to fold." I do not want to have to face that again.

Q.: *What kind of cooperation do you have from the Musicians' Union?*

Mr. Abravanel: One hundred per cent.

Q.: *Would it be fair to sum up your stay in Salt Lake City by saying that you did not find your Weimar in Europe but that you did find it in the United States and have in a way helped to create it here?*

Mr. Abravanel: This comparison is probably going a little too far. But I did help create (a) an orchestra where there was none to speak of, and (b) opera performances. We have done *Salome*, *Aïda*, and *Cavalleria*. We have a ballet, thanks to a first-rate choreographer. He is the first to say that it would not be possible without the Symphony. We have composers whose music is being played. We have chamber music. Our key men have a quartet. They also have a woodwind quintet and a brass ensemble. We have teachers because our key men have time to give instructions. We make it possible for talented young people to play with a symphony orchestra. We have the spirit of continuity. The young people know that they have a chance and they will not have to go away in order to be recognized, and the audience knows it because they are their friends. This is their orchestra.

6 THE SYMPHONY ORCHESTRA AND THE CONDUCTOR

Helen M. Thompson and Max Rudolf

Q.: *Mrs. Thompson, you have perhaps the best bird's-eye view of symphonic life in the United States today. How would you characterize it at the moment?*

HELEN M. THOMPSON: I would say that it is growing, expanding, thriving, but that it has many problems. Actually, we are carrying an inventory of some fourteen hundred organizations that classify themselves as symphony orchestras.

There are four different groups of orchestras. The first classification is what is termed "major orchestra," and that is another way of saying that there were in 1966 twenty-six orchestras in the United States—mostly in the larger cities, of course—that engaged their musicians, all professionals, on a full-time basis for a certain number of weeks per year. That length of employment will at least total twenty-two weeks of the year. A few orchestras, we are happy to say, are operating on a year-round basis (fifty-two weeks). The Honolulu Symphony has expanded its work to the point that it probably will qualify for the major-orchestra classification.

The next grouping we refer to as "metropolitan orchestra." This means that some of the musicians are employed on a full-time basis, but more of them are engaged in other work for their main source of income. As of January 1967 there were forty-seven symphony and three chamber orchestras in this classification, and it is estimated that by the end of the 1966–67 season another seven will meet the requirements. You may be amazed to discover the extent of the change in circumstances and in our thinking that came about in a brief twelve-month period, that ten additional United States orchestras in medium-sized cities increased their seasons so that they now qualify as metropolitan orchestras, an increase of nearly 35 per cent within a twelve-month period.

The classification of "urban orchestra" was established in January 1966 and refers to orchestras operating on annual expenditures of $50,000 to $100,000. As of January 1967 thirty-one orchestras had validated their qualifications for this classification, and it is anticipated that another twenty-five will have completed their requirements by the end of the 1966–67 season.

Then we come to the great mass of orchestras in this country which we refer to as "community orchestras." This means that, on the whole, most of them will have a limited number of professional musicians, and the great majority of their members are really avocational musicians.

Each of these different groups of orchestras fulfills a similar function in its own home community. When you add all of them together, plus the college orchestras, we end up with around fourteen hundred symphonic organizations.

These classifications are of no significance in themselves, of course. They merely provide us with a handy method of indicating the professional growth of our orchestras. Translated into meaningful terms, the dramatic increase in the number of orchestras now included in the major and metropolitan classification means that many more concerts are being played to more people throughout the entire land, and that more musicians are receiving increased income for their work as symphony-orchestra players.

Max Rudolf: An important question must be asked in this connection: Do orchestras grow according to the demand of the public, or are we in the process of creating demands? In line with steadily increasing activities in the field of symphonic music, we observe in many communities significant efforts to create a demand for more music. This, I think, is a typically American situation.

MRS. THOMPSON: I see the thing going forward simultaneously. We are trying to increase the length of seasons of the musicians; therefore, we are in the process of trying to build a larger audience. At the same time, I believe it is evident that there is a greater and spontaneous demand on the part of the public.

MR. RUDOLF: In order to offer extended employment to the musicians we need longer concert seasons. We also need subsidy. Although American symphony orchestras are supported privately and do not enjoy government subsidies as they exist in many countries, we are assisted by private financial support, which, after all, is a form of subsidy. On the average, wouldn't you say that orchestras earn about half of their budget?

MRS. THOMPSON: Roughly, yes.

MR. RUDOLF: The New York Philharmonic, I think, earns more than 80 per cent, but most orchestras are quite happy in earning 50 to 60 per cent of their total expenditures. In order to maintain this ratio and still extend the season, we need more interest on the part of the public. Usually this is done through drives within the community, and, more important still, by bringing music into the schools in the hope that a new generation of music lovers will grow up.

MRS. THOMPSON: Despite the fact that our orchestras date back more than a hundred years (the New York Philharmonic was formed in 1842), it seems to me that only in recent years have we really begun to learn how to use an orchestra. We have traditionally thought of a symphony orchestra as an organization that gives formal concerts at only one locale, and occasionally goes on tour. Now when we begin to jump to full-time employment concepts, which our musicians are rightfully insisting that we do, and talk about using a symphony orchestra twelve months a year, this is quite a different matter. In the first place, we have weather considerations in this country that make summer as well as winter concerts a problem. People are just not interested in packing themselves into a concert hall in 100-degree weather. Instead of bringing the children to the concert halls, the orchestras play youth programs in the schools. For this purpose the Cincinnati Symphony has been splitting the orchestra into groups, so that they can play for the children in even the smaller auditoriums.

Year-round employment for musicians opens up the whole matter of Pops concerts, outdoor concerts, specialized concerts of all kinds. We are just beginning to see that a symphony orchestra is a very usable, and can be a very flexible, organization when one begins to think of the total needs of the community and the ways in which each orchestra may fill those needs. I think that is the way we are going to expand our seasons to fifty-two weeks.

Not long ago one barely touched on the subject of federal subsidy of the orchestras, pointing out that, although the federal government offered no direct financial subsidy, many of our orchestras received financial support from their municipal governments, and a few from county or state governments. This has changed dramatically with the passage of the legislation establishing the National Council of the Arts and Humanities, which is financed jointly by the federal government and private contributions. Although the National Council program still is in its infancy, the channels and procedures have been established whereby federal governmental funds, when matched by private gifts and local and state governmental funds, may be applied to assist in the expansion of activities of symphony orchestras and other phases of the arts.

In addition to the federal arts legislation, impressive developments have taken place in federal education legislation whereby state and local education agencies are charged with the responsibility of working closely with nongovernmental arts organizations in the joint planning and development of new programs that will knit professional arts activities into the fabric of the education curricula at both student and adult levels.

A few years ago, one would have worried about the absolute necessity for taking drastic action on a national scale to assist the professional orchestras in lengthening their seasons so that their players could have year-round employment as performing musicians. But the Ford Foundation came forth with at least a partial solution. The Foundation is investing $85 million in long-term challenge grants for the development of endowment programs by the nation's professional orchestras.

Each of the approximately sixty orchestras deemed to qualify for the program will be given opportunity to establish or increase its own endowment. Within the next several years, each orchestra must raise a substantial amount of money locally, to be matched by the Ford Foundation. The income from the investment of these combined funds will help stabilize the orchestras' annual resources so that they can extend the length of their seasons, and, in so doing, materially improve the contractual arrangements they can offer to their musicians. Beginning in 1965 the Rockefeller Foundation has assisted ten or twelve orchestras to extend their seasons two to four weeks. The grants enabled the orchestras to link up with colleges and universities in their own areas in offering reading sessions and concerts devoted to works of regional and nationally known composers, in presenting symposia on contemporary music, etc.

These developments undoubtedly will affect every phase of symphony-orchestra operations and growth. The increase in numbers of concerts under these various programs is going to open up greater professional opportunities for professional development not only for the orchestra players but also for young artists, young conductors, and contemporary composers.

MR. RUDOLF: In this connection we should consider the historical background of symphonic music in the United States. In Europe it had developed in a different way. Music was offered originally as high-class entertainment by royalty and by wealthy individuals who could afford to have small symphony orchestras in their mansions. In the course of the nineteenth century all these activities were taken over by large, or even smaller, communities motivated by civic pride. There was no objection to using municipal funds to support music on a very high level, replacing, so to speak, the sponsorship that had been formerly exercised by royalty and nobility. In America, symphony orchestras as such, and particularly opera, were imported as a finished product from Europe. The wealthy in the United States in the nineteenth century, able to afford this high-class entertainment, imported the idea and indeed in many instances the performing artists, dispensing with the relatively slow development which had led to it in Europe. At this point in the United States, we have to make up for a forced growth, so to speak, which has taken place in a hothouse. Now we must undertake steps necessary for continued but more natural growth. To do this, every effort must be made to educate our young people.

Q.: *Mr. Rudolf, as musical director and conductor of the Cincinnati Symphony Orchestra, how do you allocate your time? How do you rate your tasks, beyond seeing that the orchestra remains a first-rate organization and its musical standards are kept?*

MR. RUDOLF: I try to interest more and more people in our orchestra; for instance, by addressing groups, by newspaper interviews, also by talking to individuals. In this way I hope to convince more people that something must be done fairly soon to extend the orchestra's activities. If we do not succeed in time, we cannot hope to attract first-rate musicians.

Let me explain this problem in a little detail. In looking for a musician to replace a member of the orchestra who either wants to leave or has retired, I usually find a sufficient number of wind players, but it is difficult for me to locate qualified string players. While there are people who study string instruments, the limited earning potential offered by orchestras induces many music students, after their graduation, to enter the teaching field, where, they think, they will have a better opportunity to earn enough money to raise a family and plan a secure future. So, in other words, to continue symphonic music at a high level, we have to offer equally attractive jobs.

MRS. THOMPSON: By that do you mean musicians will be paid on a fifty-two-week basis?

MR. RUDOLF: Eventually. This is now in the mind of every orchestra musician. We know that this has to happen, and we all feel that it will. During the nine years I have been active in Cincinnati, a change has taken place in the minds of the trustees. After all, they are responsible for the fate of the orchestra. They guarantee the organization financially, and while they do not interfere, I am happy to say, in any artistic planning, they are interested in the well-being of the organization as such. The board of trustees realizes fully that we must work toward year-round employment.

MRS. THOMPSON: Mr. Rudolf, your comment about the board not interfering artistically reminds me of what one of your colleagues from another orchestra said at one of our conductors' training projects. He was asked whether the board interfered artistically. He answered that during the previous year he had played approximately seventeen new American works, and the board thought that was a little too many and asked him if he could reduce the number. So he said yes, and the following year he played sixteen. I think, perhaps, that that one seventeenth is indicative of the percentage of artistic interference we get from our boards. I don't think it totals any more than that, do you?

MR. RUDOLF: My board has never told me what I should or should not play. We have discussed certain reactions on the part of subscribers and newspapers, but they do not exert the slightest degree of pressure. It might interest you to learn that a gentlemen's agreement exists between the board and myself. When I was engaged, the president of the board told me: "We think that you should have full freedom in all artistic matters within the possibilities of our budget. We will never interfere. You can play what you want, you can engage musicians as you see fit, as well as soloists, and so forth, because," he added, "we think that is the only way you can be successful. If you are not successful, we are sure you would not wish to stay."

MRS. THOMPSON: To increase the employment for the musicians or lose them to other fields, that is the very thing that is accounting for orchestras in the smaller cities operating on a quasi-professional or quasi-avocational basis, depending on your point of view. Many of the well-trained musicians go through our conservatories and colleges, and when they graduate they have to choose a career. Should they play with one of the fine orchestras which will guarantee them a modest annual income, or should they work at the college or university level where they probably would earn considerably more and receive what we call "security" or "fringe benefits"—hospitalization, medical care, retirement income, and other returns. Most finally decide to go into the teaching field. They may wind up in a community of modest size, and want to play symphonic music. So in the smaller cities there are many well-trained musicians in the orchestras who have chosen another profession for their main source of income.

MR. RUDOLF: I appreciate these efforts, but, unfortunately, this makes it more difficult for the major symphony orchestras to visit those communities regularly to present a substantial number of first-rate symphony concerts. Perhaps it is difficult in the smaller communities to achieve a happy medium between local pride and the maintenance of the highest possible level of performance, which, I think, can be offered only by professional major orchestras.

MRS. THOMPSON: I think you are absolutely right. If we look back in history, we always find this situation. There was the occasion when people in Philadelphia were very much upset because a start was made to form an orchestra there; they said there was no need for a local orchestra since the Boston Symphony was coming to Philadelphia and playing all the music they required. Well, we have the Philadelphia Orchestra and we still have the Boston Symphony.

Who is to stop anyone from starting an orchestra? No one in America can say to a group of people: "You cannot form a symphony orchestra." There is no czar of the arts, no controller of the urge to form an art museum, an orchestra, a little-theater troupe, a ballet, an opera company, and these groups simply emerge. Everything should be done to encourage them. I think they must be taught that the highest possible artistic standards should be their goal. These groups should be the leaders in bringing into their communities the best in professional performing arts, the major symphony orchestras, etc.

MR. RUDOLF: The increased activities of our orchestras must go hand in hand with an increased discernment in music. We need a larger and more discerning public. For this we need the co-operation of the schools.

In Europe the love for and understanding of music had its basis in the family. I was born in Europe, so I remember very well that a large number of people were exposed to music in the home and grew up knowing that music is something fine, something worthwhile, and, of course, went to concerts, opera, and so forth. In this country there are relatively few families where this tradition exists. Therefore, our schools are the place for expanding music education.

MRS. THOMPSON: I spend at least half of my time on this very problem of assessing what a given group is achieving. But part of this has to do with distance and size. If I am not mistaken, there are great cultural centers in Europe accessible to many, many small communities. In the United States we are talking about hundreds of miles between cities. Not long ago I was out in Montana, around the Rocky Mountains. In the whole state of Montana there are only 650,000 people. They live hundreds of miles from any major city. How many are going to drive through the blizzards and travel hundreds of miles to San Francisco or Salt Lake City to hear a concert? So what do we have in Montana? We have six of these small orchestras in a state with a population of only 650,000. I am sure they hope to grow artistically, but the fact remains that in six cities, in this really out-of-the-way part of our United States, people are exposed to live music for the first time, through the quasi-avocational orchestra. You have premières in every concert, I am sure—city premières, that is—of Beethoven, Mozart, Brahms, *et al.* That is one function, as I see it, of all this mass growth of orchestras in this country. They are bringing live music, though of not so fine quality as we might wish it, to audiences who have never been exposed to it.

MR. RUDOLF: But we must not forget that this is a large country with a huge population, and naturally this has certain consequences for our musical life. For instance, in Cincinnati we play in a music hall with 3,760 seats. As we play each program twice, we try to sell more than 7,000 seats each weekend. A large audience like this, of course, is unheard of in Europe. Still, in order to exist we must sell seats. Our Saturday-evening subscription series almost fills the house. On Friday, the situation is not so good as yet. Since we play every program for 5,000 subscribers, we must offer it on two days, and so the question arises how to fill the empty seats on Friday. Out of my Saturday-evening audience of roughly 3,000 or 3,500 listeners, I can count on 1,500 to 2,000 real music lovers—people who have as deep an understanding for the great masterworks as any European public. I wonder whether there is any European city of similar size where you have as many music lovers. Only we have to fill more seats.

MRS. THOMPSON: I imagine that a great many people do not realize that the halls in many cities in which our orchestras play are considerably larger than is the new Philharmonic Hall in

Lincoln Center in New York City. As you just said, your auditorium holds almost 1,000 more people. The New York City population is about 8 million and the Cincinnati population is half a million. The whole growth of musical interest is vital as a part of the total picture of our broad public becoming more knowledgeable in all of the arts. The orchestras have proliferated more rapidly and more successfully than almost any other field of the arts. What we are really discussing now, it seems to me, is how to take advantage of the tremendous amount of leisure time we now have in our country, partly due to the development of automation; to see to it that the public's leisure energy is directed more toward the arts in all of their phases, be it music, museums, painting, or whatever. With this evolution taking place, part of the economic situation is going to resolve itself.

Q.: *The question of subsidies has been raised; hopefully this would relieve the symphony orchestra of the task of continuing to support itself through large subscription endeavors. What are your thoughts on this?*

MR. RUDOLF: In Cincinnati, for instance, we earn about 56 per cent of our budget, which is typical for a symphony orchestra in our budget category. Our remaining income has been traditionally derived from an endowment fund plus an annual fundraising campaign.

MRS. THOMPSON: There are other subsidies than direct federal and foundation subsidies. In the first place, the federal tax program is set up so that persons who wish to make contributions or gifts to nonprofit organizations, including orchestras, may claim a special deduction from their income tax. In other words, instead of money coming into the federal government in Washington and then drifting back to the Cincinnati Symphony, for instance, the taxpayer has made his contribution directly and has told the government he has done so, and then his tax has been reduced by a certain percentage depending upon his income. In this way, the government has long subsidized every orchestra in the country, and it also does so in two other ways relating to taxes.

There was a day when all orchestras had to pay federal tax on concert admission tickets. That tax has been removed. There is also a provision whereby the orchestras are exempted from taxes on the income they receive. So in three different tax areas the federal government makes it possible for the orchestra to use funds which it otherwise would not have.

Furthermore, we are seeing a tremendous increase in the number of cities that use city funds to help support the symphony orchestras and other cultural activities. In some cases, these funds are appropriated to the general financing of the orchestra; in others, these funds are set aside by, say, the parks division for outdoor concerts, or by the public school board for concerts in the schools. Each year more cities do this.

We have two other levels of government—counties and states—that are going into the arts subsidy. Los Angeles County, which includes several cities, is a prime example of this. It has almost a million-dollar budget annually for musical events. Much of that money goes to the Los Angeles Philharmonic Orchestra and to the famed Hollywood Bowl in the summertime.

We are now also witnessing a rapid increase on the part of the states in the arts field. New York State has gone further than any other state in this, and has formed its own arts council and appropriated substantial funds for the arts. It has set the pattern, and state arts councils are beginning to appear all over the United States. As yet not very many of them have any money to spend, but they are in the planning stage.

Q.: *Do financial necessities dictate the kind of programs you are going to present?*

MR. RUDOLF: Definitely so. If half of the season's repertory would consist of contemporary music, I would lose subscribers right and left. Still, about 12 per cent of my total repertory is selected from contemporary music, and this is accepted. I think every conductor must know his community well enough to decide how far he can go, so that he can fulfill his duty toward contemporary composers and still not jeopardize the best interest of his organization. Again, this is a matter of education. I try to talk to people to convince them that they should try to keep their minds open, to listen to contemporary music. Actually, we are doing much better in this respect than our European colleagues. Compare programs and you will see that modern works are rarely heard in subscription concerts in Europe. What we need definitely in the United States is improvement of our musical programs on radio and television. In the country at large, it is mostly the FM stations that broadcast good music. This is all right, but I cannot help suspecting that not too many people listen to FM stations. What must improve is the musical climate, as I would call it.

Mrs. Thompson: The whole radio picture, bad as we often think it is, has to be balanced against the spreading ownership of large and fine recording libraries, of individuals who set their changers and settle down for two- or three-hour formal concerts at home without ever having to get out of their easy chairs.

Mr. Rudolf: But do not forget, you may be talking about 5 or 10 million people, but think of the many other millions. It will not be long before ours will be a 200-million-people nation. In Europe they have problems, too. I had bitter complaints from people over there interested in musical culture. They told me how difficult it is to interest the young people in good music. It is not only an American problem, it is a worldwide problem within our Western culture.

Q.: *Mrs. Thompson, how do we fill the need for qualified conductors?*

Mrs. Thompson: Mr. Rudolf has helped in this situation a great deal. With the broad scale of fourteen hundred orchestras, we need as many conductors, and there are hundreds of young men in this country who wish to conduct. Obviously the great majority of them are American-trained, unfortunately without too much emphasis on conducting. Mr. Rudolf and the Cincinnati Symphony have been (actually four times) participants in our special training program for conductors. Mr. Rudolf also appeared as a teacher in Baltimore at the Peabody Conservatory of Music and was in charge of a conducting course in Tanglewood. Perhaps he would like to tell us what he sees as some of the main problems in the training of conductors.

MR. RUDOLF: The training of conductors is made difficult by the lack of training ground which Europe provides in the field of opera. Most conductors start in Europe as assistant conductors with an opera company. This could be compared to an internship of young physicians. Opera companies provide an opportunity for conductors starting on their careers, first to coach singers and to assist the leading conductor in many of his activities, and finally to take over a performance. If the young conductor shows talent he will advance and, after a number of years, be offered a leading position. Opera companies lend themselves so well to conductor training, because they present between five and eight performances a week.

In this country, with our rather sporadic opportunities in the field of opera, we have to think of different methods and means, such as the workshops as they are organized by the American Symphony Orchestra League, with which Mrs. Thompson is connected. The League has done wonderful work in this respect.

I wish that more communities would follow the example of Cleveland, where sponsors have made it possible to engage a number of assistant conductors and conductor apprentices. This should be the practice of every major symphony orchestra. Conducting can only be learned by doing and observing within an organization which presents public performances. Courses in conducting at a school of music can develop conducting ability only to a certain point. From there on young musicians must be in direct touch with musical performances played in public.

MRS. THOMPSON: Do you think our whole formal educational

system is a real factor in the lack of early training for the conductor? Obviously, most of these young men go to public schools for eight years and then to high school for four years, and are eighteen or nineteen before they can enter college, at which time most of them begin seriously studying music for a minimum of four years. Then they are ready to start their career. I feel that despite all the work we have done, they do not get enough practical knowledge of conducting.

MR. RUDOLF: Very true. In spite of much pondering, I have been unable to put my finger on the real problem. I just know that many young musicians in my time started studying full scores and playing them on the piano at the age of thirteen or fourteen, and so when we entered a school of music we already had gained certain skills essential for a conducting career. The average American student, I am afraid, starts much too late.

MRS. THOMPSON: Of course, this early skill was linked with your opportunity to hear live concerts at a very young age, which many young people are not able to do in this country.

MR. RUDOLF: Yes, this is one of the main reasons.

Q.: *What induces people here to become conductors?*

MRS. THOMPSON: We are living in a period of glamorization of conductors. In the last decades conductors have become spotlighted. Many, many young people are attracted to conducting as a glamorous profession. If they spent some time around our great conductors, they would know that a great deal more hard labor goes into it than glamour. They have not thought much about conducting, and no one has sat down with these young people early in the game and said: "Look, do you know what it means? Are you prepared to study piano, to learn languages, reading of scores, and so on?" These young people flock to our workshops and begin only then to see what it means to "be" a conductor, the tremendous lifelong study, research, and work. At that point, some of them—fortunately—decide that the field of conducting is not for them.

MR. RUDOLF: To put it in general terms, there are two problems: one concerns training, the other how to make a living. Job opportunities are limited. A European opera company needs at least six conductors, including assistant conductors. As there are a great number of opera companies operating throughout the year, there are a great number of jobs available. In this country there are just not enough opportunities for conductors. As far as training is concerned, we face another difficulty: attending a school of music and working for a degree means spending a great deal of time on subject matters not directly related to music. As a conservatory student, I just studied music, nothing else. It was up to me then, up to my personal ambition and interest in other subjects, to decide how much time and effort I would devote to nonmusical studies. But my curriculum was limited to music.

MRS. THOMPSON: American community orchestras certainly provide one avenue of starting in the field of conducting. If we had master conductors on hand while the young conductors were doing their first work with the smaller city orchestras, then we would have a better training situation.

Q.: *Is there anything to be said, Mrs. Thompson, about the particular nature of the administration of a symphony orchestra?*

MRS. THOMPSON: As our orchestras begin to expand rapidly and new ones come in, the whole field of orchestra management becomes increasingly important. We have become involved in it in a number of training programs, and in the last few years something very interesting has been happening. More and more young people have been writing to us while still in college and saying: "I don't know whether to go into music or into something else. I have gone into business administration and still want to be in music. What are the chances in the world of arts with this combined background?" The last couple of years we have begun to find young people selecting this field, not just drifting into it, and deciding that they want to be orchestra managers. We have a course we give each year, and the last several years we have had grants from two foundations, more recently from the Martha Baird Rockefeller Fund for Music, to enable us to have interns in management training. There are a number of young people with different backgrounds who are being supervised by major orchestra managers, and in this way we are preparing them for their future positions. It is interesting to observe that within the last few years the number of young people with a better musical background who want to make management their career has increased considerably. This development is very exciting and encouraging.

MR. RUDOLF: I agree with you. In Cincinnati we have a young manager whom I consider extremely capable. We need that kind of well-equipped and imaginative manager in order to extend our activities and to reach the goals which I mentioned previously. But, on the other hand, the conductor must also participate in administration. Unless I took a direct and personal interest, the manager could not work efficiently. In this country, an orchestra is a business enterprise, and without some talent and inclination to participate in administration a musician cannot be successful as music director of an orchestra.

MRS. THOMPSON: I might add that we meticulously teach these young managers to work with the conductor on a teamwork basis. I think the position of the orchestra manager is changing. He must be more than a "manager" as we used to think of him. He must be a creative administrator working in concert with the artistic director.

We now have need of scores of additional trained orchestra managers and arts administrators for the new programs. The necessity to prepare adequately trained people for these posts is going to force the development of new undergraduate curricula in our colleges and universities as well as new short-term training programs at the graduate level.

The next step will be to give serious attention to the type of education needed to help the average citizen obtain better preparation for his dual role as appreciator and patron of the arts.

The responsibility of the individual citizen to continue to share in the financial support and in the leadership for the further development of our cultural life has been skillfully written into the basic plans of each of the new developments of the past twelve months. In this way, the element of voluntary individual responsibility for national growth that is so essential a part of our concept of democracy in the United States not only has been retained but is being given dramatic encouragement through the preferred recognition and assistance by national nongovernmental institutions (such as the large private philanthropic foundations) and by the federal government as well.

7 THE COMPOSER AS CONDUCTOR AND PERFORMER

Aaron Copland and Leon Kirchner

Q.: *How does a composer feel when he hears another conductor performing his music? Is it generally a satisfying experience, or do you get that urge to go up to the podium and lead the orchestra yourself?*

AARON COPLAND: I think that any composer, whenever he hears his composition performed under someone else's direction, is always curious about how his music is going to be read, so to speak. I often feel that people talk about interpretation as if there were only one correct or right or really inspired way of reading a piece of music, but I do not think that is true. Actually there are various possible ways, let us say ten different possible ways, but the eleventh way would be wrong. An interpreter ought to see a composition from his own angle, must in fact see it from his own angle, and in doing so he may uncover an aspect of the piece that the composer himself might not have been aware of. And because of that, I find it can be a very illuminating experience to hear somebody else do my own piece, even though I myself know I might do it differently. How do you feel, Leon?

LEON KIRCHNER: Somewhat the same way, although, to be sure, one rarely hears a tenth performance.

MR. COPLAND: That was just a "symbolic" ten.

MR. KIRCHNER: I am sure it was and I agree, although the concept seems unfortunately a little outdated.

75

MR. COPLAND: What is a little outdated?

MR. KIRCHNER: The idea of having ten different performances.

MR. COPLAND: Are you saying there is only one right performance?

MR. KIRCHNER: Much "music" being written today is performed once and is written to be performed but once; what you are talking about is the classical heritage.

MR. COPLAND: I am talking about the normal music we hear in the concert hall.

MR. KIRCHNER: In that sense, there is an infinite number of performances available, and this is precisely what keeps music alive. The music is so structured as to invite unusual and subtle combinations in time and space.

Q.: *Assuming that we're dealing with a great work of music, what is it that makes a great performance?*

MR. COPLAND: That is a tough question. I suppose that you are getting the essential quality of a piece of music when you hear a really good performance. Unconsciously we have in our minds an ideal performance by professional musicians, which we may never hear, against which we instinctively match the actual interpretation we do hear. Now, if I hear, for example, a slow movement of a Brahms symphony performed in a way that seems to me a bit too juicy for what I imagine Brahms was really like or felt like, I would feel that something essential in the music was being falsified. The really great interpreter has in his mind a kind of ideal performance which he is trying to reach for. Don't you feel that, Leon?

MR. KIRCHNER: Yes, that is an interesting way of putting it. The composer has his conception, the ideal, the conductor sees a part of this and conveys it to the orchestra, the orchestra in its turn conveys a part of the conductor's conception of the work, and finally the audience receives the distillation. But this is what makes music such an interesting art. I have heard performances which, although not note- or rhythm-perfect, were nevertheless extraordinary conceptions. The music was revealed in such a way as to bring out combinations hitherto unknown to me. If a performer has a profound structural conception of a work, he is capable of revealing these combinations, and by this act he prolongs the life of the music heard.

MR. COPLAND: I have become most aware of what I wanted my own music to sound like when I conduct foreign orchestras. There I have to convey what I think the American quality in my own music is, and I can immediately hear how little at home a foreign orchestra feels with American rhythms and American sentiment. For example, when I conducted in Holland, where the orchestra had very rarely played any American music, I knew immediately that there was a basic difference in approach. It is going to be quite some time before we hear our music played in Europe in a way that is really convincing, the way you can hear a Tchaikovsky symphony played in America in a truly *Russian* manner. The European orchestra has a long way to go, I fear, before we can hope to have it communicate our rhythms and our sense of discretion in the expression of emotion. The long, impassive line, without crescendo or decrescendo, is difficult to achieve with a foreign orchestra.

I remember Sergey Koussevitzky once saying to me that he always liked to watch a composer conduct his own works. You know very well that composers have a poor reputation as conductors. But Koussevitzky claimed their technical limitations did not matter—whatever they did was instructive, for he could always find something essential about the work from having watched the composer conduct it. Along the same lines he used to say to me: "You will never sell American music in the larger sense and never convince people of its value until you get American conductors to conduct it." And this by a man who had himself introduced many American works and had been complimented on what he had done with them and for them.

MR. KIRCHNER: Certainly once the language is understood, the

77

conductor has a much better conception of the work. Composers who are physically gifted can project the gesture that intrigued Koussevitzky. I find the same experience to be true on a slightly different level with students who play, however inaccurately, their own works at the piano. There is a physical thrust through which they reveal what they are after. One gets to the core, and through these physical signs the teacher is able to guide or direct the attention of the student toward the technical achievement of his "idea."

MR. COPLAND: I remember a Japanese student of mine at Tanglewood who was a very polite and kind young fellow; I was astonished when I first heard him play one of his pieces at the piano. It was extraordinarily violent. I had no idea he had such violence inside him until he sat down to play. You often get the real character behind the notes from hearing a composer and working with him. Leon, don't you think there is something essential in our American feeling for rhythm which is different from that of the European?

MR. KIRCHNER: Quite. This came up in a rather unusual way some years ago. I studied with Schoenberg, as you know, and although the "language" of my works was not foreign to Schoenberg's ear, they were, nevertheless, idiosyncratic rhythms alien to his language, and yet he picked them up, "tuned in" on them, and would go over them time and again until he caught them in his ear. This is precisely what you are talking about, Aaron. Do you know that even American performers rarely have this special awareness? Their education is essentially European, in the limited sense. They learn from their teachers, who rarely devote themselves to contemporary language, American or European; they hear and study the traditional projections of eighteenth- or nineteenth-century scores.

Q.: *Is this because our tradition does have the jazz idiom with its rhythms, or is this because we have in the twentieth century developed a peculiar rhythmic idiom that is difficult for the European to follow?*

MR. KIRCHNER: No, I think it is a rhythm which may or may not be related to the jazz idea. If you hear a French performer play Debussy and Beethoven, there seems to be an enormous difference in contact. I think you spoke of this, Aaron, when you indicated that it would be a long time before European orchestras played American music in the way our orchestras can play Tchaikovsky. Our orchestras are a melting pot of European musicians and many of our conductors received their education abroad as Europeans, whereas European orchestras are simply not the place one would expect to find an American.

MR. COPLAND: I do not quite agree with you on the subject of the origins of the Americanism of our own rhythms. I think it has a very definite relation to the fact that we all grew up with jazz rhythms as part of our natural habitat.

MR. KIRCHNER: Instinctive.

MR. COPLAND: Instinctive. But if you stop to realize what jazz does rhythmically that European music does not do, I think that you will find what Roy Harris said many years ago has a true basis, in fact; we are highly influenced in our rhythmic thinking by the fact that we are more conscious of the smaller units within a single metrical beat than the European is. I have noticed in the performance of my own works that an accomplished European performer concentrates on the phrase as a phrase, with a beginning, a middle, and an end. They are going someplace and sing a whole phrase as one thing, which is, of course, admirable. We do that too, but due to the American musician's jazz background, he will be thinking rhythmically in terms of, let us say, the separate eighth note, within a $\frac{4}{4}$ measure. It is what the jazz player does when he beats his foot in regular quarters and never plays regular quarters. He plays above and around and between those basic rhythms with a feeling for the smaller units. It is that sense of the imaginary rhythm that is always there and always controlling which is very special to us, and I think we get it by way of jazz.

MR. KIRCHNER: True, but it is still a puzzle. Stravinsky had this very quality you describe long before he knew what jazz was about.

Q.: *I have often noticed when young performers are reviewed in the metropolitan press in New York that if they give a varied program they tend to get better reviews on their contemporary music than they do on the classics, as if it were more natural for a young twenty-year-old pianist to play the music of his own time with greater surety and conviction than it is for him to be able to fit himself into an eighteenth-century mood and re-create that kind of music.*

MR. KIRCHNER: But honestly, isn't it really just about as bad?

MR. COPLAND: I have found in my own experience that, in general, performers who play music of the past badly also play contemporary works badly.

MR. KIRCHNER: They are just bad performers.

MR. COPLAND: But there is such a thing as being specially gifted in one part or another.

MR. KIRCHNER: A conductor once told me after a particularly bad performance something that impressed me very much. He said: "Just think of the first performance of a Schubert symphony; that must have been horrible."

Q.: *It seems too small a consolation, doesn't it?*

MR. KIRCHNER: If the work can survive such a performance, it has real quality.

MR. COPLAND: I once spent two hours with Gertrude Stein in the south of France when she tried to convince me that you could not ruin a masterpiece, no matter what you did to it.

MR. KIRCHNER: Provided you knew it was a masterpiece, or provided the listener knew.

MR. COPLAND: Provided it really *was* a masterpiece.

Q.: *Speaking about getting across the inner idea that you have in a composition, how do you compare the two different types of orchestras?*

MR. COPLAND: My experience would indicate that we in America have come to look for a different kind of sound from our orchestras than they do in Europe. It is a more glamorous sound; it is more brilliant; it is more precise in the jazz-band sense of precision; it has more bite. It is out to "wow" you. The European orchestras, by comparison, are more relaxed, warmer in tone, not so intent on bowling you over with the sheer excitement of performance; they can, of course, give performances exciting in their own way. It is as if they had different sound ideals in mind while performing.

I remember many years ago hearing the Chicago Symphony Orchestra play under its longtime conductor Frederick Stock. I was absolutely astonished at what I heard, for I suddenly felt that I was hearing the way orchestras must have sounded in the nineteenth century. Suddenly I realized how far we had come in developing our own idea as to the proper sound of an orchestra. Speaking in general terms of our own orchestras, if you were able to listen to them all one after the other, I think you would find that there is more emphasis on glamour and brilliance than there would be with a similar number of orchestras in Europe.

MR. KIRCHNER: That is true. There are perhaps three or four European orchestras that are certainly equal to any of our own, but having played with a number of musicians from various orchestras, one is really astonished at the quality of performers in the great American orchestra. They are limited only by the understanding of their conductor.

Q.: *Mr. Copland, would you comment on the orchestras in Japan since you have conducted there?*

MR. COPLAND: I have conducted only one Japanese orchestra, the Japan Philharmonic in Tokyo. They are a talented and enterprising group. They have an air of youthfulness about them (like most Japanese they look younger than they are). How absolutely devoted to the job they are, and how anxious they are to do really well! Most people do not realize that there are five functioning Japanese orchestras in the city of Tokyo, all going at the same time. Curiously enough they have a particular gift for string instruments.

Q.: *What does a composer expect of his audience?*

MR. COPLAND: This subject is a very serious one. How are we going to interest the big music-listening public in the music that the composers of today write? That is a very tough proposition. I do not know why. I have always felt rather depressed at the thought that music is somewhat different from all the other arts. Why is the musical public so much more recalcitrant than the public in the other arts toward contemporary idioms? There must be some good reason. It cannot be that all the contemporary composers are out of their minds and writing music completely disconnected from the kind of music that the public wants to hear. On the other hand, there is no doubt we are not reaching as many of the typical music lovers as we should like to. I do not know any other solution than to get them to sit down and listen to the stuff.

MR. KIRCHNER: You mentioned Stock before. There were times, I am told, when the Brahms symphonies he conducted were rejected by the Chicago audience hearing Brahms for the first time.

MR. COPLAND: That was true in Boston, too.

MR. KIRCHNER: But he did not care—he loved Brahms and played him over and over again until the language was understood. This is rarely done for contemporary music. That is, a new work will be done perhaps once in five years or ten years, if at all. Contemporary music is rarely given repeated performances. The audience is understandably lost and a dialogue is never sustained between work and audience. I think this is a serious problem.

MR. COPLAND: I think, Leon, you would agree that one of our problems is the fact that music has to be played to a large number of people. I do not really believe that all music is meant for everybody.

MR. KIRCHNER: True.

MR. COPLAND: I think in the field of literature they have a much clearer idea of what book is meant for what reader. The publishers know whom they are addressing when they publish a work on philosophy. They are quite aware of the difference in potential sales value when they publish a popular piece of fiction. But in the musical field there is a different situation. For example, take the ordinary symphony subscriber. The symphony orchestra is a costly operation and must have large audiences, so our music is played to more people than are ready to hear it. If we could have an audience numbering a hundred or two hundred people in symphony halls, we would, I think, not have the same problem. Unfortunately we cannot choose our audiences.

MR. KIRCHNER: This is really what happens with a composer who lives long enough to become successful. He gains a public of one or two hundred, or whatever it may be in each community, through the years of repeated listening. He has a loyal audience, an audience which understands his language, which is alert to a new performance of his work, which finds communication in his work. I surely agree that one cannot expect to have a large audience for all things.

MR. COPLAND: Yes, after all, Roger Sessions' string quartets are meant to be played to people who are musically sophisticated. You cannot expect those who want to be amused by a little music to be interested, and we should not hope they would be interested; but there is no problem there because the ordinary chamber-music lover tends to be, by nature, a more cultivated person. The real problem is at the symphony concert where you must of necessity play to thousands of people at the same time, and it is in that area where we have had most difficulty in impinging ourselves.

MR. KIRCHNER: Well, whereas you can get a small group to dedicate themselves to the solution of problems in a chamber work, it is very difficult economically to get an orchestra to do the same kind of thing.

MR. COPLAND: Exactly.

MR. KIRCHNER: It is expensive, and with all the pressures on the modern conductor, particularly vis-à-vis contemporary music, one can understand, although not agree, with the ambivalence he demonstrates toward contemporary music; and when a work fails in terms of the critics or the audience, he finds what seems to be ample support for his diffidence. But what does such a failure mean? Stock, whom we mentioned before, could easily have presumed Brahms to be a failure. He might have discontinued performing Brahms and this would have resulted in the impoverishment of the audience. We have a peculiar attitude toward success. An attention of sorts must be given contemporary efforts. The typical conductor awards ultimately the fad, the chic, the quasi-sophisticated a passing moment of guilt. Rather than develop the needed dialogue between audience and composer which can only result in the wake of dedicated efforts, he occasionally or rarely performs the great masterpieces of an age. There are leading orchestras which have until now not ever performed, let alone repeated, the major works of Schoenberg. Of course, the conductor alone cannot be totally responsible for this situation. And there have been and are conductors such as Mitropolous or Koussevitzky who have had great dedication along these lines. Whereas performers in other centuries devoted themselves largely to their contemporaries, we have an enormous repertoire to face, but I firmly believe that without the constant stimuli of well-prepared contemporary scores, the past will lose its quality as well; it depends vitally on renewed frames of reference. The catalytic forces of a contemporary masterpiece can bring revelation to the past. It works both ways and I think that the present without the referential meaning of our great traditions is equally valueless.

MR. COPLAND: What I find most discouraging is the music-listening public's over-all attitude to what it is they want to get out of music. Basically, it is very different from what the composer is thinking about when he writes his music. Rarely do you find a music lover who thinks of music as a challenge or a stimulus. Mostly you will find him hoping to be consoled by music, amused by it, interested by it, but not stirred by it in the deepest sense. The fact is that people when they go to a bookstore want to browse among most recent publications, and when they go to the theater they want to see the newest play, but the concentration on the art of the past is unique to the field of music. The plain fact is that our concert audiences are simply not looking for the same thing they are looking for in the other arts, and yet we write our works out of the same urge as the playwright and the fiction writer and the painter. We want to write music which arouses people in the same way and for the same reason; therefore, the gap between the creator and listener is really disturbing.

Q.: *I wonder if the mass media, and particularly the good-music stations, have perhaps not done us a disservice by taking this experience you describe out of the performance. What is your view of the good-music station as an instrument for educating a listener? Does it make him a better listener, or does it make him a jaded one?*

MR. KIRCHNER: Well, Artur Schnabel spoke of this matter very succinctly. He pointed out that the audience in past centuries was of a different order. The audience was made up largely of amateur performers and musicians. They had the ability to go to an instrument and play through scores, make sense of them in various ways. They had an idea of melodic and harmonic and structural patterns. They had physical contact with scores and thus were prepared to hear a performance, to have an experience which was more than superficial. The stations you speak of have performed a fine service, no question. This is necessary, too, and is one more means of developing an intimacy with the musical experience; however, it is still not a substitute for effort.

Q.: *What do you mean by effort?*

MR. KIRCHNER: I think some of the most rewarding experiences, and I am sure it is true with you, Aaron, or for that matter any of us, are when we have gotten to know a work in our own terms.

We have made, each in our own way, an effort in the analysis of this work. We have thumbed through, or played through, or read through the work; and when we know the work as an old friend, we finally attend its performance and we discover an astonishing thing. We hear what we have never heard before: combinations that are heavenly; inspired passages brought about by the characteristic pacing and profound understanding of the great performer; we have an experience which is truly extraordinary. And we know that we shall not again as an audience share this particular experience. It is rare and poetic; it is memorable. We find this kind of experience, particularly in orchestral audiences, less and less frequently. Works are, almost of necessity, administered rather than performed in this sense!

MR. COPLAND: In relation to the FM stations, I agree with Leon. They have been doing a very important job in making more serious music available; but one must add that the amount of conventional programing is discouraging. I have noted this in relation to recordings of mine which have one piece on one side and a different one on the other side. Ninety per cent of the time they will choose to broadcast the side that is frequently played, when I would much prefer them to turn over and play the less familiar side. In the old days before recordings, we used to make excuses by saying that to rehearse an unfamiliar work takes so much more time than to replay the familiar one; but that does not apply to radio stations. A mere turn of the wrist would give the public an experience of a work they do not know well. But here again the idea that music is more valuable if it is familiar than if it is unfamiliar is so well grounded in public acceptance that they just ignore what is less well known.

MR. KIRCHNER: But Aaron, how wonderful it is that they can turn the work over and find another Copland. You know, there are cases where the other side of the record is a different composer altogether, and there are cases where the composer is not represented on either side.

MR. COPLAND: Leon, you know that every composer who gets lots of performances must be in this continual state of wishing that his less well-known works were played more instead of repeated performances of the overplayed works.

MR. KIRCHNER: Would you say, Aaron, that the works for symphony orchestra have decreased enormously in the twentieth century, that is, those by major composers?

MR. COPLAND: Yes, in recent times I have heard very pessimistic things said by symphony-orchestra conductors about the fact that young composers, they believe, are not interested in writing any more for the symphony orchestra. If true, that would be very sad indeed, both for the orchestras and for the young composers. I myself cannot believe that composers could turn their backs on that magnificent instrument, the symphony orchestra, just forget about it, so to speak. But there is no doubt that at present, for many different reasons, composers are not so concerned as they once were. I can hardly view this as anything but a temporary setback.

Q.: *What do you find the young composer aiming toward? Is he composing for the smaller chamber group?*

MR. COPLAND: Yes, by and large for a group of ten or twelve performers, very variegated performers, never the same combination of instruments, with lots of emphasis on the percussion and on mandolin, guitar, vibraphone, and so forth. The vibraphone is especially a favorite instrument at the moment. The great interest is in producing sounds never before heard. The love of sound for its own sake as explored by the chamber ensemble appears to be the main preoccupation.

MR. KIRCHNER: I think quite interesting along these lines is the fact that a number of groups have been established which go from town to town, from college to college—groups of five, ten, or twelve. This seems to be a new pattern, and works are written for these new ensembles.

MR. COPLAND: Yes, recent developments, stimulated by some of the big foundations, have made it possible for a group of ten or twenty young performers to gather together for an entire year within university walls for the sole purpose of preparing music by contemporary composers of a more advanced and experimental nature. This kind of seminar in contemporary-music performance has never existed before, and it attracts specially gifted young persons with a specific interest in contemporary works to become active members of such groups. The results are really quite astonishing.

Q.: *Would you say, Mr. Copland, looking back at the state of American composition, that you hold a fairly optimistic point of view of the future, or a quasi- or semi-pessimistic one?*

MR. COPLAND: I am an optimist by nature, so I tend to be optimistic. I think the fact that there are so many more composers writing in the United States today than was true forty years ago is in itself a very hopeful sign. If you have a hundred composers working, well, there may be ten good ones; but we used to have ten and could hope for only one good one. I belong to a generation which was very stimulated by the fact that the musical scene seemed to be somehow just right and ready for us in the twenties in a way that is no longer true. I have never stopped to analyze why it is no longer true, but I sense that younger composers nowadays lack the assurance that what they are doing is brand-new for America. They work in terms of the international scene, but we were establishing something in the field of serious music that was brand-new for America.

MR. KIRCHNER: There are communities throughout the United States where the musical life is really quite vital and healthy.

MR. COPLAND: Are you thinking mostly of university circles?

MR. KIRCHNER: Many university circles.

MR. COPLAND: The universities are beginning to play a really key role in performances of contemporary music, and are supplying audiences for such music. In a sense they are doing the job the symphony orchestra used to do and no longer does.

MR. KIRCHNER: And they are developing their own symphony orchestras, too.

MR. COPLAND: I agree. That is likely to develop also.

MR. KIRCHNER: And in the next years this may prove to be the most extraordinary development on the musical scene.

8 THE ORCHESTRA MUSICIAN AND THE COMMUNITY

Tiberius Klausner

Q.: *What comments do you have to make on the position of the concertmaster?*

TIBERIUS KLAUSNER: I always like to think of the anecdote that a friend of mine once told me, describing the role of the concertmaster. He put it this way: If the concert goes well, the conductor gets the credit. If it goes badly, the concertmaster is blamed for it. Actually, though, it is an important position. The concertmaster is responsible for performing all violin solos called for in a score, and he should be able to pinch hit for a guest artist in case of emergency. He may also have his own annual solo appearance with the orchestra, as I have had, having performed fourteen different concerti during my twelve years in Kansas City. However, I am primarily the leader of the violin section and a very nice relationship between the conductor and the concertmaster can be built up on this basis. I spend many hours working on bowings. He tells me of his musical ideas and approaches, but since he himself is not a string player, we work together. I set the bowings so that the rest of the section will have them for the rehearsals. Many times I am called upon to conduct sectional rehearsals.

Q.: *Now, in your position, how far does your advising go? Who builds the programs? Are you consulted? Has the board of directors any influence on this?*

Mr. KLAUSNER: Our conductor has a very healthy relationship with the board and a free hand in programing. We have several series, and he often consults me. We also have top guest artists for the series, and he gives them a free hand to choose whatever they want to perform.

Q.: *Then comes the problem of public preference, because, after all, you do not want to play to an empty hall. Would you tell us how the matter of the public interest is handled by the Kansas City Philharmonic?*

Mr. KLAUSNER: We have to cater to the public; there is no question about it. In the regular subscription concerts where we present standard repertoire, classical repertoire, people want to hear Brahms, Beethoven, Tchaikovsky, and Mozart above all. About seven years ago we also initiated the so-called Connoisseur Concerts. There we present seldom-performed works, either modern or from the classical Baroque period. We introduce many contemporary works, in fact, even avant-garde compositions. Three years ago we had a whole evening devoted to Stockhausen and his electronic music.

Q.: *What is the reaction of the listener, inside and outside the concert hall? Do you get letters or does your orchestra receive letters? Do you feel that the public has gotten educated in the time you have been here?*

Mr. KLAUSNER: Oh, definitely. First you see it in the attendance and then in the letters criticizing or praising or demanding. The public has really supported the orchestra; I don't think ten years ago it would have been possible to introduce works by contemporary composers.

Q.: *How long is your season? How many concerts do you give? How many series do you have?*

Mr. KLAUSNER: Our season is thirty weeks long. We have the regular subscription series, consisting of twelve concerts, eight of which are repeated the next day for a different audience. Then we have the Saturday-night Connoisseur series. We have a weekly broadcast and also a series of television programs. One of the most important contributions to the community is our program of school concerts; I think it is one of the largest in the United States. We play over fifty concerts to sixty or seventy thousand children, and I think it is a wonderful thing to expose them at an early age to good music.

Q.: *What is the community's reaction to the series, particularly the series for the schoolchildren?*

MR. KLAUSNER: It is very encouraging. I think this series has contributed to the attention that the orchestra receives and to its popularity.

Q.: *Do students come to informal rehearsals?*

MR. KLAUSNER: No.

Q.: *How many weeks of employment does the average member of the orchestra have?*

MR. KLAUSNER: As I have said, the season is now thirty weeks. However, the orchestra received a Ford Foundation grant of $1,750,000, a million of which will have to be matched by the community. If this is successful, then we can look forward to longer seasons. In addition, there is a recently formed Missouri State Council on the Arts.

Q.: *What is the budget for the year?*

MR. KLAUSNER: A little over $500,000.

Q.: *As you know, only one third of the usual budget is covered by tickets, so the money has to come from elsewhere.*

MR. KLAUSNER: Exactly, people do not realize this. We now have undertaken tours. In 1965, in addition to a one-week tour, we played forty-four out-of-town concerts. During the current season we will also have a ten-day tour plus a great many out-of-town engagements.

Q.: *How big is the orchestra, and how many members go on your tours?*

MR. KLAUSNER: Ninety people. Now sometimes we add musicians, sometimes up to one hundred or one hundred ten, if the score calls for it.

Q.: *From where are the musicians recruited?*

MR. KLAUSNER: They come from all parts of the country. In fact, we have several from Europe too, but primarily they come from the United States.

Q.: *How is publicity carried out?*

MR. KLAUSNER: The newspapers cooperate very nicely as far as local publicity is concerned; however, there can never be enough publicity.

Q.: *How about music critics?*

MR. KLAUSNER: We have a new music critic, a very critical one as a matter of fact; some are happy about it, some are not; but he is doing a great service to the community by demanding better things, better quality.

Q.: *It awakens the awareness of the listener, doesn't it?*

MR. KLAUSNER: Yes.

Q.: *What are your views about the position of the musician in the community and of his responsibilities or obligations as a teacher, a cultural leader?*

MR. KLAUSNER: That is a very good question, I think. This is where we musicians have to educate the people. Although the Philharmonic alone cannot offer full-time employment, most of us, of course, have to supplement our income by accepting other employment. I teach at the university and so do many of our finer musicians in the orchestra.

Q.: *Could you tell us what your average day consists of with the symphony orchestra?*

MR. KLAUSNER: Many days we have two services, which means five hours, or one rehearsal and a concert. Since I also have a string quartet, I might have a rehearsal for the string-quartet series.

Q.: *How are the rehearsals planned? What does the orchestra have in weekly rehearsals in preparation for one program?*

MR. KLAUSNER: We have about nine services per week, which could be anything from a rehearsal to a school concert or regular concert.

Q.: *How long are the rehearsals?*

93

MR. KLAUSNER: Two and a half hours. Anything beyond is overtime.

Q.: *How long is the break?*

MR. KLAUSNER: Fifteen minutes.

Q.: *So you have very concentrated rehearsals. Do you have many section rehearsals also?*

MR. KLAUSNER: Sometimes; if it is a difficult or challenging work, we have section rehearsals, which I enjoy conducting.

Q.: *Is the orchestra very alert in reading? How does it compare with your experience with European orchestras?*

MR. KLAUSNER: I think the variety of programing broadens our experience. The Connoisseur programs really expose us to different types of reading that Brahms or Mozart would never have dreamed of, and this is what improves your reading.

Q.: *How many women are in the Kansas City Philharmonic?*

MR. KLAUSNER: Quite a few. We have several married couples. One way to attract good musicians from out of town is to offer employment to both husbands and wives, which few orchestras do. We have, I would say, at least twenty-five women.

Q.: *Do musicians accept employment outside of the musical field?*

MR. KLAUSNER: Yes, unfortunately, several have to supplement their income. One, for instance, drives a taxi; another is employed between the seasons at a tree nursery; but most of them teach and try to make a living from music. You know, it is hard. Not everyone can teach or wants to teach.

Q.: *Can the average musician in Kansas City live on the wages that he earns as a symphony musician?*

MR. KLAUSNER: I would say that for the average musician it is quite difficult to live only on the income he derives from the Philharmonic. The weekly wages are good but the season is short. If he has a family, he has to supplement the income by accepting other employment. I would also like to mention the importance and the success of the "Young Audience" program

94

in Kansas City, and the fact that many of the Philharmonic musicians participate in the various ensembles sponsored by this organization. Outside of the music field, one of our musicians has a novelty shop, one works in advertising, one works for the government as a clerk, and one works for a record shop.

Q.: *But these people have regular business hours for that. How do they fit in with the rehearsal schedule?*

MR. KLAUSNER: It is difficult during the season. They usually have an agreement with their employers that enables them to attend rehearsals.

Q.: *In your ten years with the symphony, how would you say the lot of the symphony musician with the Kansas City Philharmonic has improved? What improvements arise out of increasing community interest in the civic orchestra?*

MR. KLAUSNER: As I mentioned, the Connoisseur series would have been unheard of ten years ago. The number of school concerts has increased. Out-of-town concerts have increased, and the prestige of the musicians has grown.

Q.: *In what way do you think the musician's prestige has improved?*

MR. KLAUSNER: We play more concerts. Concerts are better attended. Television has helped too because we now have a series on TV. Weekly radio broadcasts have also helped.

Q.: *In your opinion, what does the public think of the musician? Do the listeners appreciate that the musician has very much to give to them, that he is a kind of pioneer for them?*

MR. KLAUSNER: Until not too long ago the musician was not looked upon as he was in Europe, where music carried the same prestige as medicine or any other profession. But today people are getting much more enthusiastic about culture in general; they need it more. They have become more educated regarding music and are taking the initiative.

Q.: *It is amazing to see what has happened in Kansas City in the last decade, isn't it?*

MR. KLAUSNER: Yes, a cultural awakening has taken place here and, I am sure, in many other cities.

Q.: *There are many factors that contribute to this awakening. You have given us a fascinating profile, Mr. Klausner, of the typical American symphony orchestra, that in Kansas City; and one thing which I find most interesting is the rather exquisite interrelationship the orchestra has with the community. I should like to press you a bit further on this.*

MR. KLAUSNER: One interesting thing is that, since 1964, musicians have been interviewed on some of the radio broadcasts, so that the image of the musician has tended to appear much more "down to earth" to the average listener. His profession has emerged a little more attractively also. All of this explains partly, at least, the steady growth of the attendance at all concerts, with more and more younger people in the audience. I think this is what is encouraging. Much of the credit for this is largely due to very active women's and other philharmonic committees and to various social and philanthropic organizations that sponsor balls, barn sales, and other affairs on behalf of the orchestra. In this way, the public has taken the lead, and its support has provided a solid foundation, but we need government aid too, because there is a limit as to how far we can carry it only on public support.

Q.: *Are there other musical groups in the community, besides those formed by members of the orchestra, that you believe stir up interest in symphonic music or educate this public that is so important to the American symphony orchestra?*

MR. KLAUSNER: Yes, there are several, as a matter of fact. There is a civic orchestra in Kansas City, Missouri, and one in Kansas City, Kansas. There is one in Independence, Missouri. They are all within a radius of fifteen or twenty miles. There is also a doctors' orchestra, and it is a very good one.

Q.: *Do you have a youth orchestra?*

MR. KLAUSNER: We have two. One is a training orchestra, and one actually gives a series of concerts.

Q.: *Do the teachers in the schools encourage the children to listen to the symphony?*

MR. KLAUSNER: Of course. Primarily the music teachers are the ones who expose the children and encourage the concerts we give in schools. The music teachers are responsible for preparing the children for what they are going to hear by talking about the works that we are going to perform. This is very important.

Q.: *Do you think that the audience is limited to certain social classes?*

MR. KLAUSNER: I believe times have changed. It used to be that only rich people could afford culture and demanded culture. Today "culture" is within the financial limits of everybody, provided you expose them and make them realize that the concert ticket is no more expensive than a movie or theater ticket. And if you take the people away from home, from recordings and television, they will find there is still no substitute for a live performance.

Q.: *I wonder if we might try to sum up by asking a few questions about the commitment of the musician to the community. Does the Kansas City Philharmonic have a large or small turnover of musicians at the present time, that is, musicians who do not stay on from year to year?*

MR. KLAUSNER: There is a turnover and it is rather large. But this is due to the fact that Kansas City offers a short season. Consequently people will accept better jobs if they get a better offer. However, we have been lengthening the season to make it more attractive, financially speaking. And the grant from the state of Missouri is enabling organizations such as the Kansas City Philharmonic or St. Louis Symphony or other professional groups to tour the state and play in smaller communities which, until now, were unable to bring in professional organizations.

Q.: *Is this the only orchestra performing in Kansas City, or have other professional groups been invited to come here to play?*

MR. KLAUSNER: No, this is the only orchestra series. There is a local impresario who engages artists and groups for her concert series. The university also sponsors a chamber-music series.

Q.: *Are any of the other symphony orchestras coming here?*

MR. KLAUSNER: The St. Louis Symphony was here in 1964. As a matter of fact, it was sponsored by the Kansas City Philharmonic.

Q.: *A cultural exchange?*

MR. KLAUSNER: That is right.

Q.: *It is always very interesting for the public to compare, isn't it?*

MR. KLAUSNER: Yes, of course.

Q.: *But you do feel that you have been part of a very significant and important facet of musical evolution in the Midwest, that you have come out of a European background, been trained in New York, found your place in Kansas City, have a home here and now have many, many roots in this community, and have a feeling about its evolution and growth which involves a significant amount of devotion, to say the least. Is this a fair way of summing up your present commitment to Kansas City?*

MR. KLAUSNER: Yes, it is, and I am proud that I have been able to be a part of Kansas City's cultural development.

9 THE EDUCATION OF THE ORCHESTRA MUSICIAN

Howard Hanson

Q.: *Dr. Hanson, would you tell us about the two orchestras which you have founded and with which you have been closely associated, the Eastman–Rochester Symphony Orchestra and, more recently, the Eastman Philharmonia Orchestra.*

HOWARD HANSON: These are two very interesting orchestras. The first, the Eastman–Rochester Symphony, so named because it is in the city of Rochester, New York, and because it is associated with the Eastman School of Music of the University of Rochester, is a professional orchestra. It was formed primarily for the purpose of giving performances of new works by American composers—a kind of a "composers' laboratory." I am proud of the fact that a good many young composers who took part in these "laboratory concerts" have since become famous composers. I can remember exciting first performances of early works by Aaron Copland, Roy Harris, Leo Sowerby, Bernard Rogers, Randall Thompson, and many others. As a matter of fact, in the past four decades we have performed approximately two thousand scores by over seven hundred composers!

The second purpose of the orchestra was to record important works of American composers so that it would be possible to hear their music in recordings. Over the years, we have recorded not only the music of our most distinguished contemporary composers—men like Copland, Barber, Piston, Sessions, Carter, to name only a few—but also the works of historic figures of the past—Ives, Chadwick, MacDowell, Carpenter, and the like.

The second orchestra, the Eastman Philharmonia, is quite a different orchestra. It is composed entirely of student players. No faculty members take part. The orchestra is chosen from the students of the Eastman School of Music by audition. In this orchestra there is no "seniority." If a young freshman student is the best oboist in the school, he becomes solo oboist of the Philharmonia!

This orchestra was formed for the purpose of creating an outstanding student symphony orchestra which might serve as a practical demonstration of the high standard of orchestral training in the United States. This was particularly important inasmuch as we had been invited by the Department of State, under its Cultural Presentations Program, to make an extended tour of Europe, the Near East, Poland, and Russia. It was important that this orchestra be not only technically brilliant—which indeed it was—but that it also be a bona fide student orchestra, composed *entirely* of talented young American students.

Q.: *Then one might say that you have had two functions in American orchestral history. One was to introduce the work of American composers. The other was to help with the development of American symphony musicians. Of what works do you have the most exciting memories? Do you recall a performance that stands out in your mind as having been particularly exciting because of the work which you were presenting?*

DR. HANSON: I can think of a good many. I remember vividly two works to which I have already referred. The first orchestral score of Roy Harris was obviously the work of a highly talented young man and one which presented many difficulties and challenges.

The second work was a very early score by Aaron Copland, a *Cortège Macabre,* of which we gave the first performance. It was part of a ballet entitled *Grogh,* with, as I recall, a rather macabre story. It was a highly dynamic and exciting work and I thoroughly enjoyed conducting it.

Q.: *Did you have great difficulty in persuading your musicians to play the new works when you first started presenting them?*

DR. HANSON: We had no real problems. I think that, in general, there may be among orchestral musicians some apathy toward, or even resistance to, new music. The player knows that Beethoven wrote good music, that Mozart was a good composer; he is probably happier playing music that he knows and in which he has complete confidence.

With new music one never knows whether fifty years later it will be considered a masterpiece or whether it will die within a year. The performer may hesitate to spend a great deal of time and effort on music the future of which he cannot possibly prophesy.

Q.: *I was wondering about the new works which you have performed with the student orchestra on your overseas tour and about their reception by foreign audiences.*

DR. HANSON: One of the purposes of the tour was to show the standards of orchestral training in the United States. For this reason, in addition to playing American music, we played a great deal of the "standard" repertory—Mozart, Beethoven, Schubert, and the like. Fifty years ago our symphony orchestras were composed largely of foreign-born and foreign-trained musicians. This was a good thing for the United States because many of the finest orchestral performers from Italy, France, Belgium, Germany, and Russia came to America and brought with them the distinguished discipline of their countries.

We have profited from the best of European disciplines, and as a result we have developed in the United States a great orchestral discipline of our own. We were anxious to show through this student orchestra the tremendous progress that has been made in orchestral technique. The enthusiastic response from

European audiences and from music critics justified our fondest hopes.

Q.: *You mentioned that orchestras fifty years ago were composed largely of European-trained musicians. When you formed the Eastman–Rochester Orchestra, what was the proportion of American to European musicians?*

DR. HANSON: At the beginning, for example, the concertmaster was French, the solo cellist was a Belgian, the solo horn was Russian, the first-oboe was an Englishman, and so on. Today, in contrast, every first-player in the orchestra is American-born and American-trained. This does not mean to imply that we prefer Americans in any chauvinistic sense. It does indicate that we have come of age and that it is no longer *necessary* to import orchestral players.

One of my great friends was the late Sergey Koussevitzky, for many years conductor of the Boston Symphony Orchestra. I was not only a great admirer of Dr. Koussevitzky but we were also close personal friends. He came to the Boston Symphony the same year I became director of the Eastman School, over forty years ago. He used to say that the history of American music began "when I came to Boston and you came to Rochester!"

In any case, it is true that in the twenties it was necessary for him to import from Europe most of the first-players of the Boston Symphony Orchestra. Today the situation is completely changed.

Q.: *How do you account for this tremendous development in orchestral playing in the United States?*

DR. HANSON: In addition to the development of the disciplines already referred to, an important factor is the great improvement of the instruments themselves, particularly wood winds, brass, and percussion. Today's instruments are mechanically much better. They are easier to play well than the instruments of fifty years ago.

On the tour of the Eastman Philharmonia, we noticed that in a number of countries the musicians were handicapped by the quality of their instruments. Certain of the players of provincial orchestras could, I am sure, have performed with better intonation and quality if they had had better instruments.

The second point is one to which I have already referred. In the early part of the twentieth century, we imported great performers and teachers representing the best of European performing techniques. We brought great wood-wind players from France, brass players from Germany, string players from Italy, Belgium, Austria, and Russia, and distinguished conductors from virtually every European country. They brought to this country the greatest European traditions of performance.

Our players have built upon this tradition and, in certain instances, have added new technical achievements. I would say, for example, that there is now a fantastic new American school of brass playing influenced, at least in part, by jazz, with its enormous technical demands upon the performer.

There is a third point which deserves mention. The European player was, for the most part, the product of the European conservatory. The European university, on the other hand, was apt to be disassociated from both the creative and the performing arts. The American university is frequently an "umbrella" for the arts as well as for the sciences and humanities. As a result, our American music student is educated in a somewhat different manner. His education will, in all probability, embrace a broader curriculum. This, I believe, has some influence upon his approach to esthetic problems in performance.

What we are trying to do is to give our music students as broad an education as possible. It is becoming increasingly obvious that if the arts are to develop successfully in this country the artist must become a vital part of the life of his community. The artist must not act as though he were alone on his own special planet. He must be able to talk with people, to present his ideas, to take his place in the mainstream of community life.

Q.: *I have heard complaints that the string instruments have not been improved as have the winds and brasses. Isaac Stern made the point that it was increasingly difficult each year to play "above" a modern symphony orchestra in the performance of a concerto. Do you have any comments?*

DR. HANSON: I would agree completely with Isaac Stern. It does not appear that we have been able to "improve" upon the great violinmakers of the past, although I must say that I have heard some beautiful instruments made by modern violinmakers.

The big problem for the performers of concertos for string instruments would seem to be the sheer size of today's great symphony orchestras. When the soloist is competing with one hundred ten other musicians he is at a great disadvantage unless the conductor is considerate, courteous, and discreet!

Q.: *The second complaint is from the graduate student of musicology who claims that he cannot study music and also learn to perform it. He is generally discouraged from trying to become both a scholar and a performer, and as a rule gives up performance to become a somewhat "dry" critic. Do you find this true?*

DR. HANSON: I suppose that this is true, but perhaps no more true than in any other profession. We are obviously becoming more highly specialized, whether in law, medicine, the arts, or the sciences. The demand for perfection in performance can be attained only by hours and hours of practice. The tendency for the artist to pass up scholarship and research in favor of his instrument is quite understandable, and perhaps even necessary.

On the other hand, I must say that I know a number of musicologists who have a keen interest in performance. As far as the concert artist is concerned, the demands upon him are too great to permit much time for other branches of his art.

The most serious demand, it would seem to me, is that of the public that all works must be performed or conducted from memory. The first result of this demand is an immense burden upon the performer. The second result is the stagnating effect upon the repertory. A soloist might be inclined to perform a new concerto if he could perform it "with the notes." He may not be inclined to memorize a new work which might have a first—and last—performance!

Q.: *I have heard musicians complain that none of the other faculty members have to memorize in this fashion. The teachers of English are not required to memorize everything that they teach. Why is this necessary for musicians?*

DR. HANSON: This is a development of the late nineteenth century, the cult of the virtuoso. The only field which has not yet been seriously affected is that of chamber music. It is still possible to play quartets and sonatas with the music.

Q.: *What disciplines does one find in the curriculum of a performing musician today that one might not have found thirty or forty years ago?*

DR. HANSON: The most obvious change is probably in the development of musicianship. I suppose that there have been pedagogic changes in the teaching of all instruments. These changes seem to go in waves. The most important change seems to me that the modern orchestral player is apt to know a good deal about the music which he is playing. In my early days I met some very distinguished players who were so concerned with their instrument that they did not seem to be paying much attention to the music which they were playing.

Today, on the other hand, the orchestral player is apt to be well informed about the music which he is playing—about the problems of form, counterpoint, orchestration, and the like. He will probably have a knowledge of the history of his art which would have been rare fifty years ago.

Q.: *You mentioned that one of the primary objectives of the tour of the Eastman Philharmonia was to show the difference in the training of the young musician in this country and abroad. What do you feel are the important differences?*

DR. HANSON: The great problem in Europe is that many of the

countries have not yet recovered from the great wars which they have suffered in this century. The result, in certain instances, has been a kind of cultural "displacement" which has affected adversely their cultural life. The critics commented particularly upon the tremendous technical competence and discipline of our young musicians and upon the musical knowledge and understanding which characterized their performances.

Q.: *Do you have any outstanding reminiscences of your tour of Europe, the Near East, and Soviet Russia?*

DR. HANSON: We have a great many. We began our tour in Portugal and Spain and went as far north as Sweden. We then crossed the Alps and played in Athens, Cairo, Alexandria, Nicosia, Beirut, Ankara, Izmir, Istanbul, and Aleppo. We recrossed the Alps to West Berlin and then on to Poland and a final month in Russia.

The most exciting experience for me personally was in Syria. I had received a letter from the American ambassador in Damascus informing me that the Syrians had never heard their national anthem played by a full symphony orchestra. Could I possibly orchestrate and perform it? The concert was only two days away and the idea seemed impossible. However, I was so intrigued with the idea that I called in our librarian and told him that if he would be willing to stay up all night and copy the parts I would stay up all night and orchestrate it! Two days later the Syrians heard their national anthem for the first time in a symphonic arrangement! I have been told that my orchestration of the Syrian national anthem is still used to begin and end the broadcasting day. I do hope that this is true. It would be a claim to immortality, and my contribution to a great people.

Q.: *What did you learn from this experience with a great student orchestra that you might not have learned in dealing with a purely professional orchestra?*

DR. HANSON: In the first place, we found that our high opinion of the standard of the American student was justified. In a number of cities the statement was made that this student orchestra was the equal of their professional orchestras. In one of the most important cities which we visited, a principal critic wrote that, after hearing this American student orchestra perform so brilliantly, the Europeans might well restudy their whole attitude toward music education.

In the second place, we reaffirmed our belief in the communicative power of music. This was beautifully illustrated in our final concert in Leningrad. The Hall of Nobles was packed, with hundreds standing. We had played at least eight encores and the audience would not let us go.

Finally, because we had to take a midnight train to Moscow, we left the stage. I retired to my dressing room to change when I heard a continuing rumble from the auditorium. I slipped on my overcoat and went to see what was happening. To my amazement, I saw this great audience standing and applauding an empty stage. My associate conductor and I went to the stage to express our appreciation, whereupon the entire audience rushed to the stage, the men shaking our hands and the women presenting small bouquets of flowers. It was without doubt the most touching experience of my life and the most eloquent testimony to the communicative power of music.

10 THE UNIVERSITY SYMPHONY ORCHESTRA

Wilfred C. Bain

The education of all qualified students is a major objective of the people of the United States. This educational objective is organized to include eight years of elementary school, four years of secondary school, four years of undergraduate education at the higher-education level, and one to three or more years of graduate education. The completion of these levels entitles a student to a diploma or an academic degree. The degrees are designated as the baccalaureate, earned after four years of study at the higher-education level; the master's, after five years; and the doctorate, after seven or more years. Licensing to practice medicine or law, for example, or to teach in the elementary or secondary schools requires additional examinations or the completion of specific courses of study.

It has been said that the education of its people is the largest and most important industry in the United States. More persons participate in this industry than in any other single endeavor. More money is spent on education than on any other aspect of our society. There are now over two thousand colleges and universities in the United States. Their individual enrollments range from a few hundred to forty thousand and more. The course-study offerings of these colleges and universities range through the spectrum of man's knowledge. Most of these higher institutions offer instruction for academic credit in some form of music study.

Such courses will include both the study of music as a language, literature, and grammar and in performance. The study of music as a language will include both its creative and recreative aspects; it will also include history and the grammar and structural aspects of music. The study of music through performance includes learning the skills required to be able to perform the literature both solo and ensemble. These various aspects of music study may be combined into a curriculum designed to prepare the student for a professional career in music. Such careers are found in the fields of performance, teaching, of musicology, of composing, or of musician merchandising or managing. The colleges and universities offering music study have themselves privately and mutually organized a national accrediting agency to serve in setting and maintaining minimum standards of instruction. This agency, known as the National Association of Schools of Music, has approximately three hundred institutional members. The National Association approves or accredits the work of those institutions, including the curriculum and degrees offered by schools having a minimum of twenty-five full-time music students preparing themselves for careers in music. The National Association approves institutions for membership in this agency solely through examination.

A 1964 survey by the American Symphony Orchestra League indicates that there are at least two hundred ninety-five symphony orchestras in colleges or universities in the United States. To be listed on this roster, the college or university orchestra must be organized to rehearse and to perform on some regular basis. This number is but a small segment of the total number of orchestras in the country today—there are over fourteen hundred. In 1900, there were only thirty; in 1920, there were one hundred; and in 1940, about seven hundred. Twenty-six of these fourteen hundred orchestras had been designated by the American Symphony Orchestra League as "major" orchestras, operating on an annual budget of not less than $250,000. Twenty-four were "metropolitan" orchestras, having a budget of not less than $100,000. One may conclude from this that the symphony orchestra is at the very core of concert music in America.

Two hundred ninety-five college and university orchestras have memberships representing the classical instrumentation, that is, strings, winds, and percussion. This, of course, is minimal. Most college and university orchestras will have a sufficient number of instrumentalists to perform adequately the music of the late romantic and contemporary composers. The personnel of the college and university orchestra is composed principally of students pursuing curricula leading to academic degrees in music. Not all players will be majoring in music, however. Talented amateurs in the academic community, professors from other disciplines and their families often use the participation in the university orchestra as a form of recreation. Where the college or university orchestra is lacking in key players, the music faculty often participates in the rehearsals and performances. This is done to furnish to the students with the orchestral experience of a minimum standard and to serve as a performance model.

The educational objective of the college and university orchestra is to teach the orchestral repertoire through performance as well as to provide the academic community with cultural enjoyment. In most institutions educating musicians, orchestral participation is required as a laboratory experience for all students majoring in an orchestral instrument. In most universities abroad, music study at the university is confined to the study of music history, acoustics, and composition. The study of the performance of music is assigned to special schools—the conservatory, the Hochschule, the single-purpose college of music. In the United States, the tendency is to offer the disciplines of music theory, literature, and musical performance in a single educational institution. The musicologist is not a scholar or historian only; he is required to be a performer as well. With this educational objective in view, instruction at the advanced level is offered in all the orchestral and band instruments as a principal field of study.

The student, however, may not ordinarily devote more than 40 per cent of his total study time to one field of performance study. As a music major, he is required to take studies in the language and literature of music; the theory of music, its grammar, syntax, and structure; and the history of music, its styles, analysis, and literature. In addition, the student must spend some time studying general subjects. Such a curriculum pattern is considered well rounded, but sharpened in one area. Since inevitably there are many varied patterns of organization of the college and the university orchestra, it might be interesting to cite one university as a prototype.

The School of Music at Indiana University is one of eleven colleges and schools in the university. The university is a state-tax-supported institution located in Bloomington, Indiana, and has a very large number of students majoring in music. The university has an over-all enrollment of approximately twenty-four thousand students on its principal campus in Bloomington, with a total enrollment of over thirty-four thousand—including those on the regional campuses. The first semester (September to January) of the academic year 1965–66 showed an enrollment of more than fourteen hundred full-time music majors. The school faculty numbers one hundred twenty-seven full-time teachers with the ranks of professor, associate professor, assistant professor, or instructor. The orchestra and instrument faculty has five teachers of violin, two teachers of viola, three of cello, and one of double bass. In the winds, there are two teachers of flute, one of oboe, two of clarinet, two of bassoon, three of trumpet, two of trombone, two of horn, and one of tuba. There are two teachers of percussion. All are full-time instructors and they devote themselves to teaching their particular instrumental skill and literature.

Many of these teachers were formerly first-chair players in the country's major orchestras. There are not less than two hundred fifty student instrumentalists, playing in four different orchestras with no duplication of any of the players. No faculty members are assigned to playing in these orchestras. A weekly rehearsal schedule is intensive and extensive. Orchestras 1, 2, 3, and 4 rehearse two hours two days per week. These orchestras are then divided into two large orchestras, the Philharmonic Orchestra and the Repertoire Orchestra. The Philharmonic plays six major concerts per year and accompanies the annual performance of the School of Music's production of Wagner's *Parsifal*. In 1966, the School of Music presented its eighteenth annual production of this opera.

The Repertoire Orchestra plays children's concerts for the community and reads extensively. Both the Philharmonic and the Repertoire orchestras rehearse two hours two days per week. The total rehearsing done by the average instrumentalist assigned to one of the four orchestras and the Philharmonic or Repertoire orchestra will average eight hours per week.

The Philharmonic Orchestra plays the usual solo literature. The program played in November 1965 included the following: a *Faust* Overture of Richard Wagner, the First Essay for Orchestra of Samuel Barber, and the Symphony No. 4 in G major of Gustav Mahler. Other works performed by the orchestras during the forty-sixth season include Bartók's Concerto for Orchestra; Beethoven's Piano Concerto No. 3, op. 37; Beethoven's Symphony No. 8, op. 93; Brahms's Symphony No. 4; Copland's *Billy the Kid;* Mozart's Piano Concerto in C Minor, K. 491; Prokofiev's Symphony No. 6; Strauss's *Till Eulenspiegel's Merry Pranks* (*Till Eulenspiegel's lustige Streiche*); Tchaikovsky's Symphony No. 4; and Stravinsky's Symphony in C.

Orchestras 1, 2, 3, and 4 have a regular performance schedule composed of one or two operas, a ballet, and a concert comprising overtures, concert piano and strings or wind, and compositions by student composers of the school.

The 1964–65 year, which includes the summer session, scheduled a total of forty-one performances of eight operas. The purpose of this extensive and intensive program of music-making is to prepare the prospective professional for his position as an employed paid musician in the professional world. The standard repertoire must be learned prior to the entrance of the prospective professional to a professional post. The orchestral activity at the student level is truly a music laboratory for the student.

Who conducts these orchestras? The conductors are regular members of the faculty chosen from those who have had extensive professional experience as conductors. Four conductors are assigned to conduct the six orchestras. No one conductor serves in one musical medium only. All conduct symphony, opera, ballet, concerti, and student compositions. The students majoring in conducting are assigned to rehearse and conduct a single piece in one of the concerts of Orchestras 1, 2, 3, or 4, or to conduct the fourth and fifth performances of one of the operas. Every attempt is made to simulate the rehearsal conditions and procedures followed by a professional orchestra. There are a set number of hours set aside for the rehearsing of the music for each concert, opera, or ballet. This is carefully calculated when the repertoire is chosen before the beginning of the performance season.

The rehearsal schedule for the academic year is planned and approved by the administration of the School of Music, by the faculty committee on the orchestras, and finally by the instrumental faculty as a whole. The various conductors are assigned to specific concerts and they propose a repertoire for the solo orchestras. The operas are chosen by the opera staff, the ballet by the ballet and opera staff working together. All of these proposals must have the agreement of the various committees and the administration before the beginning of the season.

The instrumental faculty is responsible for choosing the personnel for most of the orchestral positions. The conductors enter into this phase of the selection and organization of the orchestras only if inadequacies appear in the various orchestral sections. This procedure prevents any one conductor from securing for himself all the best players in the School of Music. The emphasis, therefore, is placed on the ensemble and its players and not necessarily on the conductor.

The concerts of the Philharmonic are rebroadcast and occasionally a video tape is made of a special concert. Such was the case when a concert of Latin American music conducted by a guest conductor from Argentina was taped for distribution by the USIA and the Voice of America. This concert and taping were done on May 1, 1964, in Washington, D.C.

What goes on at Indiana University in the orchestral study is more or less typical of what happens in most American colleges and universities. Various educational situations dictate various patterns of organization. Some of these include a joining of players from town and gown. Others include the student in a semiprofessional metropolitan orchestral session. Few students receive payment for their participation in such semiprofessional orchestras. It is a well-established principle that one is not paid to learn; one's payment is in the training and experience one receives and in the academic credits one is awarded. It should be pointed out, however, that not all students of this curriculum will become professional players. Only a small portion of the players will eventually find their way into the professional ranks. The remainder of the student players will have learned a musical repertoire, developed individual playing techniques, with its attending disciplines, and will have sharpened and matured musical judgments for use in all kinds of musical endeavors, both amateur and professional. The theory of learning by doing is a basic tenet in this organized study of orchestral instruments at the college and university level.

11 INNOVATIONS: ACOUSTICS AND SEATING

Leopold Stokowski

Q.: *Leopold Stokowski is going to discuss three facets of his pioneering experiences in the development of American symphonies: the formation of orchestras, his novel experiments in seating symphony orchestras, and his study of acoustics of concert halls. Dr. Stokowski, first would you tell when did you first conceive of the idea of forming an entirely new youth orchestra?*

LEOPOLD STOKOWSKI: It was a little before I left Philadelphia. I was making a tour with the Philadelphia Orchestra across the United States to the Coast and back. Whenever we stayed overnight after a concert, young players would come to me the next day and ask: "Would you give me an audition? Will you hear me play?" and, of course, I said yes. I was amazed to find the tremendous wealth of talented young men and women across the land. When I returned from the tour I was firmly convinced that something must be done about this. I noticed that many of these young men and women who were so talented were very lonely. They were living in cities where perhaps they were the only ones who had the same taste in music and felt the same love for a certain instrument. They needed to find an outlet for their talents and their love for an instrument. Gradually the idea grew to form the All-American Youth Orchestra.

I did form it by going across the United States again, this time with an associate conductor—who was a friend—to assist me. On this trip, I listened to more players. I wanted to have a representative player from each state. When I finally completed all that work and came back, I formed the orchestra, and in two weeks of rehearsal made it ready for our first tour. We traveled by ship, staying on it down the coast of South America and back. We would play concerts in the cities and then come back to live on the ship—the ship was our hotel. Through the kindness of the captain, we were able to rehearse every day in the dining room, so as to keep the playing of the orchestra up to the highest possible pitch. These young players were extraordinary. It was a wonderful orchestra. Unfortunately, the next year after we had made a second tour across the United States and Canada and back to the Coast, World War II broke out. We lost our players in the orchestra, even the girls; they went off to do war work. It is interesting to note that the young men and women in that orchestra were about equally talented—women have their place in symphony orchestras, too. So that is how it began.

About nine years ago, I began to receive letters from young men and women saying, "I have graduated from one of the major music schools in the United States. I wish to enter the musical life of my country but I have no opportunity." This went on and on. Again I felt that something must be done about this. So I began giving auditions again in New York City; I do that now every day. Every afternoon I give four auditions, and I am finding a tremendous wealth of young talent—young men and women from ages of, say, about nineteen to about twenty-nine with great talent and plenty of it. We have a long waiting list for every player in the orchestra; four years ago we began the American Symphony Orchestra, and we are now giving our concerts in New York City, including Sunday concerts at Carnegie Hall, and also in cities like Washington.

Q.: *The country has gained a great deal from your efforts in*

*this direction. What have you yourself learned as a conse-
quence of this novel experience in founding two new orchestras? What would you say you have learned about the American musician or the American audience from this endeavor
on your part?*

MR. STOKOWSKI: I have learned one thing, that the young women
in the orchestra are just as talented, just as devoted to their instruments as the young men. You should see the waiting list for
violin alone.

Q.: *Are the people on the list all musicians you have auditioned?*

MR. STOKOWSKI: Yes, I have auditioned people for all the instruments. There is an immense amount of musical talent now in
the United States, but I learned from other sources that there
is an equally great amount of talent in architecture, in mathe-
matics, in engineering, and in the sciences generally. We have
now a young generation which is going to make the America of
tomorrow and we can be very proud of it. But we must give this
young generation opportunities. They are well educated, but
when their formal education is completed and they wish to begin
to work, so many of them cannot find an outlet for their talents
and their interests. If we do not give them an opportunity, they
are going to become despondent and give up and do some other
kind of work just so that they will not starve. Then fifteen or
twenty years from now, we will be the losers. So if we give them
a chance, the future will be brilliant and wonderful. If we do
not, the future will be shameful, and it will be our fault.

Q.: *What would you say about the quality of the young musician today as compared with what you may have encountered
twenty-five years ago or in your European experience?*

MR. STOKOWSKI: The quality is the same all over the world. I
travel a great deal, and everywhere I conduct I find a wonderful
young generation growing up. I do not know why it is so, perhaps
good education, partly good living conditions, but it must be

something more than that. Frankly, I do not understand it, but I look forward with confidence to the future.

Q.: *What would you say is the leeway for new orchestras in the United States? You have founded a new orchestra in New York City from musicians drawn from all over the United States, I presume. What do you think are the country's capabilities for supporting new symphony orchestras?*

MR. STOKOWSKI: The conditions are very good because we have now in the United States more than one thousand symphony orchestras. Some of them are completely professional, some are completely amateur, and some are partly amateur and partly professional. The interest in music is growing enormously. Of course, in these amateur orchestras, the players support themselves by holding other jobs; then they come home at night and practice their instruments because they are so interested and want to prepare for the next rehearsal and next concert. And this shows the depth of their love for music and for their instrument. This is going to become more widespread, I imagine; in a few years we will have more than two thousand such orchestras.

Now comes the problem of where to find good conductors for these orchestras, and it is a very difficult one. I know we have plenty of potentially fine conductors, but they have not been given enough opportunity as yet. The reason is this: if one wishes to play the piano and make it one's life work, it is not too difficult to reach a piano; but if one wishes to conduct a symphony orchestra, it is extremely difficult to practice the instrument, the symphony orchestra, because a large orchestra is very costly. It consists of from eighty to one hundred twenty players, and the managers of such orchestras do not feel they can risk giving a young, unknown conductor concerts. There is our difficulty in developing the talents which exist already among young conductors, both men and women. I see no reason why women should not be conductors; they are good actresses and good ballet dancers. Why should they not be good conductors?

Q.: *Maestro, is it your opinion that an orchestra is the instrument of a conductor, that it must reflect his will and personality?*

MR. STOKOWSKI: No, it is not. This is what I think. We have on one side of us the composers; let us take Beethoven as an example. On the other side, we have the listeners, the audience. Our duty and our privilege is to try to convey from the composer the message that is in his music. Now a great artist like Beethoven was an inspired man, and the inspiration in his music we must put into our performance. We have the score, a great mass of notes on paper. But that is not music; that is only the best he could do to make a permanent sketch of his ideas. It must always be remembered that our methods of musical notations are extremely limited. There are hundreds of things in music which we all know and do and love which cannot be written down with our notations. We have to have an instinctive feel of how music should sound. We must try to have in ourselves the inspiration that was in Beethoven as we play his music, and to convey that to the listeners, to the public. The only way I think that this can be attained is by perfect cooperation between all the players in the orchestra and the conductor. We call it ensemble. But it is a form of cooperation, the only way music should be made.

Q.: *To what do you attribute your success in taking the young players, or players who have not been together before, and welding them into this ensemble?*

MR. STOKOWSKI: First of all, the players must play their instruments well. They must have mastery of their instruments. They must be good solo players, but solo playing is one thing and orchestral playing is quite another. During the rehearsals what we try to do is to make clear the technical methods that are necessary for ensemble playing in symphonic music as opposed to the technical methods of solo playing. So, if we can find good soloists and can persuade them to cooperate, soon we begin to have a good ensemble. But it is not easy. Orchestral playing is very difficult and orchestral conducting is even more so.

Q.: *This provides us a very good opportunity to move to the second subject, the seating of orchestras. What are your views on this?*

MR. STOKOWSKI: Something very simple and strangely overlooked is that every instrument in the orchestra emits a tone in a certain direction. For example, the tone of the French horn goes to the right of the player and downward. From the tuba, the tone goes to the left of the player and upward—exactly the opposite. Now this direction of tone from the instrument is a fact, a very important fact, that is often overlooked. As a further example, in the double bass the tone goes to the right of the player and outward. The cello looks like a small double bass, but the tone goes from the cello forward. From the violin, the tone rises upward and to the right. The flute's tone goes directly upward from the instrument. The tone of the trombone and trumpet goes forward from the instrument. So, obviously, all these instruments have different directions of tone, and it is my idea that we should so place the players and the instruments on the stage that the tone goes to the listener in the audience, because the concerts are for the listeners and not for us. What we conductors enjoy most, frankly, is rehearsing. I like the rehearsals more than the concerts. There is something tremendously interesting in gradually forming things in the rehearsal. In a concert, however, the tone should go to the listeners in the audience. The tone waves should blend in the air. They travel from the stage and from the orchestra toward the listeners, and this can best be done if one studies the direction of tone from each instrument. That is why I do not place the players on the stage in what is known as the "classical" way, the way our grandfathers and great-grandfathers did. There is a foolish attitude of resistance to new ideas which we find in every form of life, not only in music. The moment someone comes along with a new idea, there are always people who resist it merely because it is new, not because it is not good. It is simply a matter of good sense to seat the players and their instruments on the stage in such a way that the instruments' tone goes to the audience and blends in the air as it travels.

Q.: *When did you first become dissatisfied with the conventional classical seating arrangements in the symphony orchestra? I recall hearing that in the mid-thirties while with the Philadelphia Orchestra you were already experimenting with new seating arrangements.*

MR. STOKOWSKI: I observed it gradually and gradually made the changes. I find that I always learn something at every rehearsal. I observe new possibilities and I make notes of them in the margin of the score so as not to forget. In Philadelphia I was always noticing that the tones did not blend well and in the right proportion. There was not the right balance between the instruments. Then I began to ask myself how I could make that balance better, nearer to the ideal. These ideas came gradually. Now I feel we have nearly reached the optimum. Unless I see some new possibilities, I shall continue to place the instruments and the players on the stage in the way I am doing it now.

Q.: *I have here a review of one of your concerts in Washington, D.C., by Paul Hume of the Washington* Post *in which he speaks of your seating arrangement as being different from any in his particular experience but one which he describes as working beautifully. "If the proof of any seating plan is the resulting clarity, balance, and tone, the Stokowski plan is excellent," says Hume. Is this the plan you have now finally fixed upon?*

MR. STOKOWSKI: Yes, approximately. Often the wood-wind instruments, which are very delicate instruments, are placed in the back center of the stage. That makes it difficult for the tone of those instruments to penetrate out into the hall and they are sometimes inclined a little to force the tone; therefore I brought them forward. On the left side of the stage are the strings, on the right side are the wood winds so that they can play even the most delicate passages without forcing the tone. The brasses we place in the back of the stage because they easily come out, the same way with the battery. The percussion instruments are in the back of the stage because they have great power, but the harp and the celesta are put forward on the stage because they are delicate instruments.

Q.: *Have these arrangements of yours been adopted widely by other conductors in the United States?*

MR. STOKOWSKI: I believe not.

Q.: *Would it be unfair to ask why not?*

MR. STOKOWSKI: I think it would be a very good question to ask the other conductors.

Q.: *I am fully aware of the fact that you have not only experimented with the seating arrangement but that you have gone a great length into this matter of acoustics, and I even recall the introduction of the acoustical shell in the Academy of Music in Philadelphia. Was this interest of yours one that developed along with your interest in the seating arrangements?*

MR. STOKOWSKI: I think it is just plain common sense. After all, music is sound. The way music reaches the listeners in the audience is of extreme importance. That was why in Philadelphia, long ago, we made an acoustical reflector on the stage. Now all over the world, new concert halls, some good and some bad, are being built. The persons who build the halls say that acoustics is just a tossup, that there is no science of sound. That is not quite true. There is a science of sound and we know a little about it, but only a very little. What we do not know about the science of sound is enormous. Perhaps in time we shall learn those things. But there is another kind of knowledge—empirical knowledge of sound—and that is what the really gifted players in the orchestras have. They have an immense and critical knowledge of sound.

Now when concert halls are built, the first consideration should be sound acoustics, obviously. If you are going to make a car, it must run. If you are going to build a plane, it must lift off the earth and climb into the air. If you build a concert hall, the first consideration should be sound and second, looks, comfort, and so on. The first requisite always must be good acoustics, good sound. Architects could learn in fifteen minutes from a violin. The violin is really a wooden box, a resonator. It has four strings, and the bow sets the strings in vibration. As the strings vibrate, they reach the bridge. They set the bridge in vibration and the bridge carries the vibration down to the front wooden plate of the violin. Underneath that plate is a sound peg which carries the vibrations to the back plate, so the front plate and the back plate vibrate harmoniously together. Inside of that resonating box is air space. On the front plate of each violin are what are called the sound holes. They lie on the side of the bridge. The air inside of the violin also vibrates; it comes out and blends with the vibrations of the front and back plate. This goes to the listeners. We have never found a better material for sound than wood, although, perhaps, someday we shall find a better material. Concert halls could be built of steel and plaster, everything that is necessary to make them strong, but if the walls on each side could be of wood, rather thin wood, like the front plate of a violin with an air space back of it connected to the concrete walls (the air space needs to be only two inches wide), that would permit the wooden surface to vibrate in sympathy with the music being played on the stage and by reflection, so the tone waves would be carried to the listeners. The wood could be made fire-resistant and then we would have natural, good acoustics.

Q.: *Maestro, you have collaborated with the Bell Telephone Laboratories in this matter. Is this knowledge of yours the result of some scientific inquiries that you have conducted with them, or is it the result of your own vast experience going back to the Academy of Music in Philadelphia?*

MR. STOKOWSKI: Both. The Bell Laboratories were kind enough to let me study with them; later I went to Paris and Berlin and studied also acoustical and electronic questions. It seems to me that it just makes sense for us to build concert halls which bring the music of the great masters particularly to the young generation. If the young generation hears, for example, the symphonies of Beethoven with the high tones much too strong and the low tones much too weak, they hear it in a form which is distorted and they become accustomed to hearing it that way. And they do not realize that they are hearing distorted versions of Beethoven or any of the great masters. That is to be deplored.

Q.: *What are your thoughts about the new Lincoln Center, Maestro?*

MR. STOKOWSKI: I would be very glad to answer that. I went to the first concert of the New York Philharmonic; I heard the orchestra play under the new improvements which had been made during the previous summer. I felt it was immensely better than it had been. What was back of the stage and the side of the stage had been removed and a single wall had been placed there, and the acoustics were much improved.

Q.: *I think that concludes rather well the matter of seating and acoustics. You have spoken with considerable optimism about the young musician, and your waiting lists contain a tremendous encyclopedia of names that could potentially belong to your symphony orchestras. At the same time, I infer from what you say that there is a great deal of conversation on the part of architects in adapting to the new knowledge of acoustics that has come out of your long years of experimentation and study. I wonder if I could ask you about how you view the future, particularly if we were to include the matter of compositions for the symphony orchestra in the general discussion. Let us look at the upcoming musician, the prospects for new and enlightened conductors, and the possibilities of new compositions. In short, how do you view the future of the American symphony orchestra?*

MR. STOKOWSKI: To return to the question of conductors: the conductors who like to continue the so-called classical seating of the orchestra have a perfect right to their opinion. In my opinion, they should continue to place the orchestras on the stage in a classical manner, if that is the way they feel they can best produce the music and convey from the composer to the listener the message of the music. I use the word "message," but it is a very poor term; I do not know a word in the English language which expresses what is conveyed by music.

Q.: *One final question: Where do you think that this process of educating can best take place, educating the ear of the public to new compositions, that is? Do you feel that this will occur through the urban symphony orchestras, through the universities, or elsewhere?*

MR. STOKOWSKI: I do not think education will do it. I think it is a question of the inner cultural growth of the individual. Education should teach us facts; but this inner growth, perception, sensitivity, is something the individual has to develop for himself. It will take time. We have now in the United States three and a half centuries of culture. But a country like Italy has twenty centuries, back to the Roman times, even to the Etruscan culture. That is as early as the Greek culture. I do not know, but possibly our cultural roots are in the Egyptian culture. All these things take time; they cannot be hurried. They are profound states of personal evolution.

12 PLAYING SYMPHONIC MUSIC ON RADIO

Martin Bookspan

Q.: *In the European radio stations there is a quite active symphonic life at the present time. How does this compare with the United States? Do we employ musicians and integrate them into radio programing, as in the case of Europe?*

MARTIN BOOKSPAN: Unfortunately, the answer to the question is no; and it is a categorical no. We always like to think in terms of the progress being made by American radio and television. In this instance, there has not been progress but regression. Not too many years ago—twelve, fourteen, sixteen years ago—there were large symphony orchestras on the staffs of the three great American radio networks, the American Broadcasting Company, the National Broadcasting Company, and the Columbia Broadcasting System. Of course, the best-known orchestra and probably one of the greatest orchestras the world has ever known was the NBC Symphony, which was formed especially for Arturo Toscanini—formed for Toscanini to rehearse and perform for broadcast only.

There were, of course, some concert performances for which audiences paid admission, which were given in various New York concert halls; and the NBC Symphony Orchestra made several tours, not only of the United States but also of South America. I do not think the NBC Symphony ever toured Europe, but this orchestra which existed primarily for the purpose of broadcasting symphonic music was disbanded. Along with the disbanding of the NBC Symphony came the slow disintegration of the ABC Symphony Orchestra and the CBS Symphony Orchestra. Now, of course, there were reasons for this regression which, I think, are best explained by the peculiar economics of American broadcasting and telecasting. The American broadcast industry is just that; it is an industry. Although the air waves are licensed by the government, it was determined by the executives of the broadcast industry that the money spent for the maintenance of symphony orchestras was, perhaps, better spent elsewhere. There are still sizable numbers of musicians in the employ of American broadcasting; all three major radio and television networks still have on their staffs some extraordinarily fine musicians, but unfortunately the musicians are not used to the best advantage. There is nothing as solid, as dependable, and indeed as musically extraordinary as existed in the American network picture a dozen or more years ago.

With respect to symphonic music, European radio and television is in the glorious period which American radio was in until roughly the early fifties—that is, the European radio, which, of course, is government-supported, can number among its employees probably the finest musicians on the European continent. The European radio orchestras are among the finest to be heard anywhere. They have plenty of time to rehearse. They are only obliged to serve for radio concerts, so their repertory can be shaped in a far more interesting form than if it would depend on sponsorship from private sources.

Also, the European musician has security. He is a respected member of society. He has not only a year-round job, he has a job for his lifetime. Here then is a situation where we in American broadcasting, or those in American broadcasting specifically concerned in the transmission of good music, are extremely envious of our European colleagues.

Primarily it boils down to a matter of dollars and cents. It is as fundamentally simple as that. Where the European radio is a government-operated enterprise, there are tax money and other kinds of support which come to the existing European radio operations. The European listener has to pay a monthly fee the better part of which is used for the programs for the radio.

I think eventually in this country there will probably be some kind of extra-industry support for American radio and television. A little later we will probably discuss the area of American educational broadcasting, both radio and television.

Q.: *I wonder if you would explain in a bit more detail the difference between the American networks and the present European radio system?*

MR. BOOKSPAN: There are three major radio and television networks which have stations affiliated with their programing across the country. One can travel from the East Coast to the West Coast and from the northern Canadian border to the southern Mexican border and find stations in every community which are affiliated with any one of the three major American networks and carry the programs of those networks. These networks exist and operate solely on the basis of their income derived from commercial advertising. It is not too difficult from that definition to come to the conclusion that the advertiser who supports broadcasting and telecasting, or whose money makes possible programs, will want to reach the largest possible audience. I suppose the next conclusion is inevitable also; if he must reach the largest possible audience with his advertising message so that the audience will go out and buy his product, then the advertiser, by and large, will be interested in program material which will have an appeal for the widest possible number of listeners.

From this comes a conclusion which American advertisers came to long ago: that program material of rather not too elevated a taste, of rather not too intellectual a content, and of a completely broad mass appeal is the program fare with which he, the advertiser, wants to be associated. Here, I think, basically is the fundamental strength and weakness of American broadcasting. As we hope to develop in our discussion, there are ways and means of reaching the minority listener, a job which is being done by educational radio and television and by commercial enterprises such as the good-music stations, of which, fortunately, we have a great many in this country.

Q.: *Would you care to discuss "The Third Program" of the British Broadcasting Corporation (BBC) in this connection?*

MR. BOOKSPAN: Yes, of course. "The Third Program" carved out for itself the mission of appealing to the most elevated taste, the most cultured listener on a many-faceted program policy. BBC 3 presented extremely fine dramatic programs, news analyses in depth and with a great deal of historical perspective and, of course, music broadcasting of the most sincere, most intensive, and even most daring sort.

Q.: *But couldn't we think of a parallel here? What are the better-music stations doing here?*

MR. BOOKSPAN: Well, here again everything must be seen in the framework and perspective of the continued existence of American broadcasting. There is that terrible word which we have used several times—"commercial." A radio station in this country, if it is not an educational or listener-sponsored station, exists or ceases to exist on the strength or weakness of its annual income from commercial advertising. This is true even for the enlightened good-music operations which must be able to show a financial profit at the end of the year. Otherwise, after a few years the station is going to have to do some very serious thinking. Either it closes up shop or does something to attract more advertisers. As I mentioned before, there are a number of good-music broadcasters, both AM and FM radio stations, but you must always remember that the station's competitive place is determined by the number of listeners it attracts. A station cannot afford to appeal to a fractionalized minority of what is already a minority audience. This is a dilemma constantly confronting enlightened broadcasters in this country. It is a tight-rope that all of us walk, some of us with trepidation. We wish that there was a way that we could be as idealistic as we would like to be yet at the same time continue to exist. Bitter experience shows that we must be very careful in our programing attitudes and philosophies.

Q.: *Would you explain about our good-music programs, which seem to have taken up some of the lag that has been created by the disappearance of the radio symphony orchestras in the United States?*

MR. BOOKSPAN: I should be happy to. Of course, the operation with which I am most familiar, and chauvinistically, about which I will speak more than others, is WQXR, which is owned and operated by *The New York Times*. It is the first such radio station to have come into existence in this country, about thirty years ago now, in the mid-thirties. It has served as the model for many such operations throughout the country. There are good-music stations in every large metropolitan area, and in some cities where you would not expect them. What these stations do basically is to broadcast recordings of fine music. I say basically, but not exclusively. There are some American symphony orchestras, the Boston Symphony and the Cleveland Orchestra are two significant examples, which have arranged with the American Musicians' Union and their own personnel for the taping of their concerts. Those tapes are then distributed to radio stations, which purchase them from the orchestras. The moneys are paid to the orchestras and then the orchestras do any one of several things.

In the case of the Boston Symphony, the association which receives the money from the radio stations then makes a sizable contribution to the pension fund of the musicians. These concerts are played by many good-music stations, in some cases very soon after the actual live performance in the concert hall. In other cases, there is perhaps a six- or eight-week delay.

Now there is one orchestra, the New York Philharmonic, which broadcasts its concerts on a specially arranged radio network, and broadcasts them live for the most part. A few stations on the Philharmonic network tape and then play the concert at a later date. The concerts are played in Philharmonic Hall in New York on Saturday evenings at 8:30, and there are, perhaps, seventy-odd stations around the country which carry those broadcasts.

There are some good-music stations which have musicians on their own staff. WQXR used to have a string quartet, but that is no longer the case. We do have a two-piano team which plays a half hour recital each week. I think there are some stations on the West Coast, too, which employ musicians specifically for the purpose of playing broadcast concerts for their listeners.

Q.: *Do you find Frequency Modulation (FM) stations in other parts of the world?*

MR. BOOKSPAN: I think so, although certainly not to the extent we have them in this country.

Q.: *Would you tell us about WQXR's stereophonic broadcasts?*

MR. BOOKSPAN: We broadcast a very substantial output in stereo.

Q.: *Do you think there is a future in it?*

MR. BOOKSPAN: We think so. We find that listeners more and more are equipping themselves with stereo receivers.

Q.: *Would you explain what stereo means?*

MR. BOOKSPAN: If I try to define anything technically, I am way over my head because I am not at all a technician. Briefly, the broadcasting of stereo allows the listener a finer transmission of finer characteristics; stereo is better able to sort out individual strands from a complex score.

Q.: *Another dimension?*

MR. BOOKSPAN: Another dimension, yes. Of course, two speakers are necessary for stereo reception and there is a complicated amplifier situation involved, but basically it is an enhancement and improvement, a more exciting means of transmitting and listening to good music.

Q.: *What are the guidelines of programing for good-music stations?*

MR. BOOKSPAN: We try to present the broad spectrum of the

musical culture of Western civilization in a most attractive manner. We at WQXR try to identify all schools of musical history, all kinds of musical compositions from the days of the Renaissance right up to contemporaries. Of course, the radical extremes are programed very carefully and almost apprehensively because we realize that there is a very small percentage of our audience that (a) is interested in this kind of music, and (b) can assimilate it and make any kind of sense out of it; but we feel that within the framework of our operation we must represent everything that is happening in music.

Q.: *Would you tell us about the response of the audience as a factor in program building?*

MR. BOOKSPAN: We have a very articulate audience, particularly when they are displeased. One rarely hears from them when they are happy, when they hear something which leaves them full of delight and exalted; but when something happens that they are not happy about, they make their unhappiness known to us.

We are very fortunate at WQXR in having a signal that covers a fairly wide geographical area; people even send telegrams from Pennsylvania, Canada, and other places which are on the fringe of our signal. But people in those places developed a habit of listening to us. Through a process of inference, if we know what our listeners do not like, we know rather well what they do like.

Q.: *But do you go along with their likes and dislikes? Do you regard your programing as a responsibility to the public, as a partially educational operation?*

MR. BOOKSPAN: Basically, we must program for the greatest general acceptance. It gets back again to the same old dollars-and-cents situation. If too many listeners are offended too many times, they are just not going to bother to tune us in anymore. If they do not listen to us, the advertiser will suffer and eventually will leave WQXR. If enough advertisers leave there will be no longer a WQXR; there is no question.

Q.: *That brings us to the problem of future music education*

*in radio. We remember when Walter Damrosch started his
educational symphonic broadcasts.*

MR. BOOKSPAN: Well, even within the rather cold, hard framework that I described, the commercial framework, there has almost always been a sense of responsibility by broadcasters, a responsibility to the minority listener, the listener with a more
elevated taste. Starting way back, I think in the earliest days of
American network radio, there were programs that aimed at a
higher level. The already mentioned Damrosch programs were
extremely fine. They were broadcast by one of America's leading
networks, the National Broadcasting Company. Walter Damrosch
—the venerable conductor who did much extraordinary work in
American musical life for fifty years in New York City as conductor of the New York Symphony Orchestra—played programs
specifically designed for audiences of youngsters. And by youngsters I mean really young people, seven, eight, nine, and ten years
old. These programs were carried directly into the classrooms
of grammar schools, and I guess this trend which the Damrosch
broadcast started continues right up to the present time. They
were made specially alive by his piano examples and by his
charm and quiet wit. He was a very warm gentleman, with a re-
markably sharp personality, and I think these broadcasts were
wonderful for their time and for what they accomplished.

Today, of course, on commercial television, four times a year,
there are the Young People's Concerts of the New York Philharmonic under Leonard Bernstein. For the past half a dozen years
these programs have had commercial sponsorship by, in one case,
a leading American oil concern and currently by one of the
telephone organizations in this country.

Q.: *You mentioned the division of the media in this connection. At first television hurt broadcasting. Now I think that
radio has recovered, because, as you said, music is meant to
be heard. Do you agree?*

MR. BOOKSPAN: Yes, you are quite right. The radio industry felt a tremendous shock in the early stages of the emergence of television—such a shock, as a matter of fact, that radio stations around the country deserted their network affiliations in droves. Before the introduction of television NBC had 250 stations or thereabouts. Perhaps as many as half of those stations decided that the radio network no longer had anything to offer them; these stations broke away from the network, programed their time completely on their own, and so hoped to appeal more broadly to their own local communities. I think, though, that the period of shock has now been successfully weathered by the radio-broadcasting industry. There are many more radio stations now programing themselves completely rather than relying completely on network programing; and the American radio station today, by and large, is in much better shape than it was fifteen or twenty years ago.

Q.: *Wasn't there a similar experience with the first appearance of stereo recordings against high fidelity?*

MR. BOOKSPAN: Not to the same extent. As a matter of fact, largely there has been a leveling off of stereo. On our own stereo programing we have tried to educate the public to the understanding of what stereo broadcasting is. Yet we still receive a good many questions regarding the transmission of stereo. Does this mean that the person who is not equipped at home to receive stereo does not get the broadcast? Does the listener without stereo-receiving equipment lose out in any significant way? Of course the answer is no; he is not getting the extra dimension which a stereo receiver would give him, but he still receives an excellent non-stereophonic signal.

Q.: *Shouldn't we be mostly concerned with the sense of performance?*

MR. BOOKSPAN: Absolutely. This, after all, is the basic and fundamental element in music-making. The technical advances, the extension of the limits of fidelity, are pluses; but basic and fundamental is the quality of the performance.

Q.: *This raises a very basic question of live performances, and I wonder what good broadcast music has done for live performances. Do more people go to concerts today because of WQXR, for example?*

MR. BOOKSPAN: We firmly believe so, and statistics back us up. The concert managements, for their part, have two different attitudes. You will often find performing organizations and managements hesitant about allowing the broadcasting of their performances because they feel that if a listener at home knows that he can hear this performance in the comfort of his favorite chair, with his favorite liquid refreshment easily at hand, then he will not bother to leave home and go to the concert hall. On the other hand, there are others who feel very strongly, and I subscribe to this philosophy completely, that nothing can take the place of actual concert-hall excitement. There is a very special kind of situation which one finds in a concert hall that cannot be duplicated by a broadcast or recording, no matter how expertly the transmission is accomplished. It is the same thing as sitting in front of a television set or in front of a radio set and watching or hearing a football game as opposed to actually being there, being caught up in excitement, in the general participation which one feels as a member of the spectator audience.

In order to get dynamic excitement and personal involvement and the personality of the artist, one must actually be present at the live performance. After all, music is made by people, and it is the personality of the performer which establishes the communication between what happens on the stage and the person who is in the audience. This is something which can only be experienced by physically attending the concert. At best, the broadcast transmits to the listener something of the sensation of what the music that is being made in the concert hall is like.

Q.: *Would you tell us about cooperation in transmitting concerts on a worldwide range?*

MR. BOOKSPAN: Basically, as far as the United States is concerned, the most meaningful work in this respect has been done by the educational radio and television operators. NET, the National Educational Television network, had a series of televised symphony concerts by orchestras in many cities in this country and in Europe; as a matter of fact, whenever a foreign orchestra comes to the United States for a tour, I understand that NET tries to videotape a concert performance and then distributes that program to the more than one hundred stations of the NET network in this country.

I guess now that we have touched on the subject of educational radio and television, it is worth spending a few words on it. This, I feel, is perhaps the ultimate answer for the specialized listener. Without the commercial pressures which the commercial broadcasters must feel, the whole area of educational radio and television is free to program for the specialized listener in a much less constricted fashion than the commercial broadcaster.

13 PUTTING SYMPHONY ORCHESTRAS ON TELEVISION

Curtis Davis

The state of the art of presenting the American orchestra on television is something which, it seems to me, had its beginnings back around the time when Arturo Toscanini was appearing with the NBC Symphony, which had a notable radio history and which made appearances on television for NBC for two or three seasons in the late forties. And the producers at that period ended up really with a very simple solution. They left Mr. Toscanini on the screen practically all the time, which for purposes of history and for the student of music is very valuable, because we are able to see what Toscanini looked like, studying a good deal of his technique as a conductor through the kinescope recordings that remain of those programs. But whenever the cameras turned their attention to the orchestra itself, we generally get a series of more or less equal long and medium shots that are of relatively little help, simple shots panning the total orchestra and not revealing in any particular way what is going on. That aspect of the development of television and its treatment of the orchestra is, I feel, the most interesting one over the past fifteen or more years.

The development of the form of the program itself was perhaps most notable at the time when the very first Leonard Bernstein telecast was given for "Omnibus" in the mid-fifties. That was the broadcast in which Mr. Bernstein analyzed, took apart, and put back together the Beethoven Fifth Symphony. There were a great many resources available to Bernstein at that time which had not been tried before in the handling of an orchestra on television. He not only had the orchestra at his disposal at all times, he could step to another part of the studio, sit down at the piano, and demonstrate the Beethoven Sketch Books, some of Beethoven's ideas for the symphony before it took final form; he could take pages of the score and analyze the way Beethoven's musical handwriting helps reveal the problems with which he wrestled in achieving a finished work. He made use of the finale to the Fourth Movement as Beethoven originally sketched it and then went through two or three revisions before presenting with the orchestra Beethoven's final version. Mr. Bernstein was even able to take the page of the full orchestra score which was blown up to almost the size of the studio floor and place himself and certain principal performers, first-desk players, on the various bar lines of the score to indicate where in the physical layout of the score the various instrumental parts lie. This really characterizes the main difference between the two types of programs that there have been on television in the past fifteen or more years.

NET, National Educational Television, has been engaged for a number of years in the presentation of broadcasts of orchestras, beginning with a series with the Boston Symphony, and since 1962–63 covering the activities of many orchestras, primarily American but occasionally also visiting foreign ones. Over the course of the past few years, we have presented some thirty hours of programing of more than a dozen orchestras; the broadcasts were generally taped during scheduled appearances of the orchestra, scheduled subscription concerts before live audiences.

There is no one solution to the presentation of an orchestra. For that reason, as a producer I have made use of the talents of several different directors over the course of the production of NET's series. There are many problems to be solved in attempting to cover any orchestra in a regular performing situation, and every new hall poses new difficulties. There are many points of view about camera placement, camera activity, the whole problem of the psychology of covering an orchestra for television.

The problem, I think, can perhaps be summarized or pointed out by taking two specific examples. In dealing with the Houston Symphony not too long ago in a concert under its music director, Sir John Barbirolli, we had a program of Mozart, Brahms, and Ravel. It was not only a question of deciding what to show at any given moment but how to achieve visually a stylistic difference that would in some sense correspond to the stylistic difference between Mozart, Brahms, and Ravel.

The solutions, without going into a great many technical details, included such decisions as using no dissolves in Mozart, dissolves being a technical term for the blending of one image slowly into another, instead of a direct cut from one image to another. In other words, in Mozart we always cut from one picture to the next. In the Brahms Third Symphony, we used primarily cuts in the first and last movements but introduced dissolves and some differences in the use of camera movement and of the 20-millimeter lens in the second and third movements.

In the Ravel, the cutting technique was a good deal more active. We also took a good many more chances in the Ravel—we tried shots that were more extreme, closeups that were more close, movements across and from one part of the orchestra to another that extend some distance farther than what we had tried up to that point. And in all of this we tried to find ways of developing visual style that corresponded to the music being presented.

The other aspect which television presents in a way that no other medium can is the work of the conductor. Observing really outstanding conductors at work, we can see that shaping a performance is an enormously stimulating and instructive experience. For example, we did a program with George Szell and the Cleveland Symphony and one of the works was the "Variations on a Theme" of Hindemith by William Walton. The work ends with a very simple major chord written for the entire orchestra. Mr. Szell, however, shaped this and the camera could watch him do it, sustaining the chord but bringing up first the winds more prominently, then taking them down and bringing up the brasses, taking them down and bringing up the entire string body, blending them all back in together. Watching Szell do this in a camera shot which was roughly from the waist to the top of his head gave us an opportunity to see the musician at work in a form which not even the rear desks of the strings, let us say, could observe as closely. Only the very first desk players could possibly see what the viewer at home had a chance to see.

There is another aspect of bringing the symphony orchestra to television which I think deserves particular stress, and that is the presentation of major orchestras from various parts of the country to the entire country, indeed to the world. One of the things which has been occurring as a result of NET's service is a gradually increasing awareness throughout the United States of the extraordinary level of musical culture achieved by a great many orchestras, not just what the music profession refers to as the East Coast Big Three, or Diamond Tiara Orchestras. One of the instances of this came most strongly to my mind on a visit to Helsinki to plan a major documentary program on Sibelius which NET broadcast as part of the one hundredth anniversary year.

For the celebration festival in Helsinki one of the scheduled visiting orchestras was the Cleveland Orchestra under Mr. Szell. Ticket sales had unfortunately not gone very well, while on the other hand ticket sales for the local orchestra, the Helsinki City Symphony and Helsinki Radio Orchestra, had gone very well indeed. They were practically sold out. We had fortunately broadcast the Cleveland Orchestra in the Sibelius Fourth Symphony the year before, which we made available to Finnish Broadcasting without charge for broadcast in advance of the arrival of the orchestra in an attempt to encourage more interest in the visit of the Cleveland Symphony in Helsinki. The fact of the matter is that the level of orchestral discipline, the performance level achieved by this orchestra is one of the most notable cultural phenomena anywhere in the United States; and I think that the audience which came to hear the Cleveland Orchestra was undoubtedly startled by what actually took place on that stage.

Over the past five years we have worked with about ten American orchestras and a number of visiting orchestras. We shall continue this with other orchestras as well as repeating some of our past programs in the expectation that we will eventually build a library to demonstrate the high level that can be achieved in this field by orchestras which otherwise might be known only to their own communities. This is perhaps because the orchestra is not led by an illustrious star conductor who automatically means record sales or because its reputation as an orchestra by name, whether Philadelphia or otherwise, only assures a certain level of sales.

NET is not bound by these considerations, which is fortunate for us and is one of the reasons we have enjoyed such astonishing cooperation from AFM, the American Federation of Musicians. Indeed the AFM created a special rate structure for NET to undertake this project. In conversations with AFM, we discovered that unless the musicians' unions, representing the interests of the musicians, made it economically feasible for NET to undertake a series of this kind, there was no point in carrying the idea further.

There are always great qualms on the part of musicians as to whether the lights are going to make it impossible for them to perform, or whether they will be an invasion of privacy. Many orchestras, indeed most of these orchestras, have never been presented on television before, never come in contact with television until NET moved with its crews and equipment. Perhaps the comment of the players of the Houston Symphony is worth noting. We taped them in a pair of concerts, identical concerts. Therefore we were present with all our gear and equipment at the first concert. At the second concert, the orchestra played under its normal setup without television present. Loud complaints were heard from musicians that the lighting was very poor for the second concert. They really wished that the lighting that had been used for television had been brought back.

This, I think, is one of the reasons why we have been asked to come back to the places where we have already produced concerts. There are, of course, circumstances under which one can bring an orchestra into a studio to perform for television especially. There are advantages in greater flexibility in the placement and use of cameras. There are also disadvantages, principally the relative limitation in acoustics within the average television studio. The rather dry sound has to be considered, if one is to approximate anything like the richness of a good concert hall.

The sound problem is complicated by the fact that in the home the television receiver, generally speaking, is not very sophisticated in its sound equipment. Speakers are small, the amplification system is relatively limited, and manufacturers have not yet given the attention to this side of it that has been devoted to the hi-fi system which has had remarkable success over the past fifteen or more years but has not yet spread to television. I think some of the concentration on color television has been responsible here, and now that color television seems solidly established, undoubtedly the next step manufacturers will take will be to increase the resources in the home sound system from the television receiver. Once this occurs and once the picture becomes something different from what we now know—that is,

142

not a twenty-one-inch screen but, let us say, a forty- or fifty-inch screen designed for hanging on the wall, something closer to the motion-picture screen—a number of things will become possible in the treatment of the orchestra on television which have not been heretofore possible.

Partly because of the limitation of the medium technically, we have not yet been able to solve the problem of showing the orchestra in its total relationship of parts, and this is one of the problems that the producer and director must work on most strenuously in coming years. This will become more possible with the improvement of the resources of the medium.

In showing the orchestra and the relationship of the parts of the orchestra, one of the kinds of programing that is of the greatest value, at least for the viewer, is coverage of the rehearsal. This is another area in which I expect NET will become more active in coming years. The problem of covering a rehearsal with camera is compounded by the fact that the conductor does stop and start again and the director must be fast enough to be able to pick up the spot in the score to which the conductor has returned as quickly as the musicians themselves do. The orchestra rehearsal is also a more complex sound problem because the relative balance between comments that the conductor may make and the musical output of orchestra is difficult to equalize.

In my own experience here, perhaps, the taping with Sir John Barbirolli, one of the occasions on which we covered and taped the rehearsal segments, was especially notable. Barbirolli's rehearsal technique involves very frequent interruptions and going back over particularly difficult knotty passages (and this could as readily occur in Mozart as in Stravinsky). Going back over it many times in order to get the adjustment just so, Barbirolli had a way of walking around, stepping off the podium, consulting with his first-desk players, and it became almost impossible for camera and for mikes to follow him as freely as we would have liked. This would be more controllable in the studio situation.

The orchestras with which NET has had the privilege of working, and we have already mentioned Boston, Los Angeles, Houston, and Cleveland, include such other orchestras as the Utah Symphony under Maestro Abravanel; the Detroit, which was conducted by a guest conductor in our taping (Thomas Shippers in fact made his United States television debut on NET); the Pittsburgh, under Mr. Steinberg; the Minneapolis Symphony, under Skrowaczewski; the Baltimore, under Peter Herman Adler; the San Francisco, under Maestro Jordá; the National Symphony in Washington; and we have also worked with such visiting orchestras as the Warsaw Philharmonic with Rowicki, the Vienna Symphony with Sawallisch, and the Royal Philharmonic, under Sargent. We hope to cover eventually the twenty-five or thirty major American orchestras and as many of the visiting orchestras as possible, though hopefully on that side our work will be extended to the European continent and Far East. We hope to originate broadcasts in homes of foreign orchestras and to bring into the American television context a sense of the place and time, the importance to the community of the home orchestra. Seeing the Amsterdam Concertgebouw directly from the concerts is something terribly important to the Dutch and is something that, I think, can be conveyed by television for American viewers in a way that would be perhaps not quite as strong if it were simply a matter of covering a guest appearance by the Amsterdam Concertgebouw at Symphony Hall in Boston, for instance. Hopefully, the same thing can be done eventually from the Far East. A concert by the Tokyo Philharmonic, for example, would be a very desirable thing for us to have.

In the opposite direction, that is to say the export of American programing to Europe, in my opinion is something that must increase in the years to come. I am afraid that most of the programing exported from the United States comes from commercial television and does not include the cultural broadcasting, partly because there is no active sales force attempting to place American cultural broadcasting overseas, but also because the foreign broadcaster has a certain pride of authorship in his own cultural broadcasting. The foreign broadcasters—the BBC, the RAI, and the German television—are extremely active in their own cultural broadcasts and find relatively little occasion to bring the work of other broadcasters, except perhaps occasionally through Euro-vision, into their own countries.

I think a program such as the one we taped with Leopold Stokowski on the world première of the Fourth Symphony by the pioneer American composer Charles Ives might well prove to be one of the most interesting of our potentially exportable programs. This is an extraordinary piece written before and during World War I, foreshadowing many of the modern compositional techniques, including aleatory writing, the whole sense of music partly by chance. At one point it calls for three conductors simultaneously when the orchestra divides into three different tempi and three different bar signatures, which one conductor simply cannot coordinate.

Maestro Stokowski said on our program: "Some people may think one conductor is already too much, but in this case three were hardly enough." It was a fascinating experience and a most important musical event in the United States for a work which had waited fifty years to have its world première. Mr. Ives's previous symphony, the Third Symphony, which had been composed in 1902–4, waited almost the same length of time to have its world première (1946), and the following year it received the Pulitzer Prize. I think there is no doubt that there would be a lively interest abroad in this sort of performance and it is another side of what can be done here in cultural exchange beyond an awareness of a level of musical performance. American composers, by and large, are not performed very much abroad and not even terribly well known. Perhaps George Gershwin is an exception, and Aaron Copland is becoming more and more an exception, but many composers who appear regularly on the programs of symphony orchestras and recitalists in this country just do not appear on the program of foreign orchestras or foreign recitalists. Perhaps television can help to make them better known through this kind of program exchange.

With NET's own programing in the field of orchestra broadcasts there are fortunately no sponsors; there are no requirements of box office; there is the requirement first and foremost of serving real audience interest and a real audience need. The kinds of programing choices that NET makes in this field cover a wide range, a far wider range in fact than it is possible for commercial television. In 1964, on the one hand, the broadcast with Leontyne Price and the Baltimore Symphony was a natural. Everyone had been waiting for some time to see Miss Price in a major performance on television since her astonishing appearance on the NBC Opera in *Tosca* and *The Magic Flute,* and this was in fact her major television appearance since that time. She presented a most taxing program, singing for about forty minutes, and the program drew extraordinary audience response all over the country.

But perhaps the sleeper, the unexpected success in the symphony schedule, was a program with Karl Heinz Stockhausen and the Buffalo Philharmonic. This was not Mr. Stockhausen's first appearance in the United States but it was the first time he and his music had been seen together on American television. This involved the première of a work of his called "Moments." The farseeing programing attitude of Lukas Foss, the new music director of the Buffalo Philharmonic, was responsible for bringing Mr. Stockhausen up there; NET not only included a performance of "Moments" itself but also excerpts from rehearsal, comments by Stockhausen himself in conversation with Lukas Foss, and some material related to the unusual notation system that Stockhausen has developed in order to make possible performances of the kind of music he conceives. All of this, leading up to the performance of "Moments," placed a rather difficult new score in a context that made it more accessible to a general audience.

Not long after that broadcast had been on the air, I found myself in Boston preparing a different program altogether, a program with Igor Stravinsky. When I arrived at the airport, I hailed a taxi and asked the driver to drop me off at the studios of Channel 2, WGBH, which is the educational-television station in Boston. The taxi driver knew the address without my having to tell him, and I remarked: "Well, I gather that from time to time you watch the educational channel." He replied: "Oh, yes, I watch it from time to time." Then I asked: "What have you seen on it lately?"—thinking he might perhaps have viewed a program like "The French Chef" (which his wife might have tuned in and which is very popular around the country). He said that the Friday before he had watched a program of music from Buffalo. He thought it was on some German composer by the name of Stockhaus, but he could not quite remember what it was. In any case, he said it was very different from anything he had ever experienced. I asked him how long he had stayed tuned. He answered: "I couldn't turn the set off." Then he asked me: "Would you mind telling me what it was all about?" I replied: "I would prefer to let the composer tell you what it is all about. He is much better qualified." But the fact of the matter is that my cabdriver had tuned in that program of his own volition. He was not a modern-music devotee in any sense, but evidently the name of Stockhausen must have rung some kind of bell for him, and he thought he would tune in to see what was going on, and he got interested in the program and watched to the end. What he made of Mr. Stockhausen's "Moments" is rather difficult for me to say, but there is an interested public for this kind of broadcasting at absolutely every level of background and education. The response that we get from our affiliates and the letters they receive from the viewing public only confirm this. It is one of the reasons why our programing is not limited to the standard eighteenth- and nineteenth-century traditional symphonic fare.

The major musical performing artists will make appearances on NET programs, sometimes performing in ways that they would prefer not to on commercial television. I think, perhaps, coming back to Leontyne Price, this may be one reason why she agreed to make this appearance. Miss Price was being presented in a very full evening, in music that she deeply cared about: a Mozart cantata (otherwise very rarely performed); the Letter Scene from *Eugene Onegin,* a role which she had just done at the Metropolitan for the first time; a scene from the second act of *Die aegyptische Helena* of Strauss, extraordinarily sung and containing something she was very proud to show off—a high C sharp. This full evening ended with an encore of *Vissi d'Arte.* Had this been an appearance for Ed Sullivan she would only have sung *Vissi d'Arte.*

Generally speaking, the symphony concert on television is somewhat shorter than it is in the concert hall. The staying power of the symphony orchestra on television is a little bit less than it is in the concert hall. The sound is less good. The picture after an hour begins to be inevitably a little repetitious, and even with a program in which it is possible to incorporate rehearsal elements and comments by a composer, I think by the time one goes much beyond an hour one begins to reach the point of no return for the television broadcast. I think ninety minutes is the absolute outside for an orchestra broadcast on television.

The aspect of education, both for adults and for young people, is something which television can serve and which, of course, educational television in the United States is serving constantly. The typical educational station devotes its daytime hours to classroom programing, which generally is brought into primary and secondary classrooms in the community which it serves. And then toward the latter part of the afternoon, the station turns its schedule over to local news broadcasts, programs for children, and then finally in the evening to programing for a general adult audience. NET's programs are made available to these stations primarily for evening broadcast, but a great deal of what we do has application for the classroom as well and can be made use of in this way, particularly by those stations which take a NET program and broadcast it at several different times during the week.

A program like the Stockhausen, for example, might very well make its appearance on a Friday evening but be repeated on the following Monday morning and Tuesday afternoon, so that those schools interested in making the work of the major contemporary composer available to their students could in this way use the program as required viewing.

This is an extension of the educational system which holds enormous promise for the future, not only because it extends the resources of the teacher but also because it makes available certain kinds of experiences which are simply unavailable to students in any other way. Even with the astonishing rise of the American orchestra, there are still many places where a student cannot attend the concert himself and has no real idea what the symphony orchestra is like, what it does. In this area the broadcaster has a job to do.

I think that it is also possible that younger composers will be encouraged by the presence of contemporary music on television to write for the medium, perhaps to develop works which are especially suited to the needs of television as opposed to recordings and radio. And the help which foundations have given to symphony orchestras very generously over the past years may very well be extended in this area.

There has been quite a remarkable explosion in all fields of activity—writing, painting, music. This is only one of many such projects that NET expects to engage in. Hopefully this will induce the commercial broadcaster to overcome some of the limitations that have held him back from activity in this area. Indeed, I think NET would welcome the competition.

14 CULTURAL EXCHANGE WITH OTHER COUNTRIES

Julius Bloom

In this chapter I will discuss some of the broader aspects of what is commonly called international cultural exchange, with particular emphasis on and reference to cultural exchange in the field of music. The expression "cultural exchange" sounds a little formidable. It also sounds like something of recent coinage, but those who probe a bit into the earlier pages of history will realize that cultural exchange or interchange among nations can be traced virtually to the beginnings of civilized society. Think back, for example, to the influx from Greece to Rome of philosophers and other intellectuals as well as artists, musicians, and writers, and indeed it was through such an influx that the later culture of Rome was able to prosper, thanks to the influence of an older culture and of more established ideas. Or think back to the later interchange between Venice, which was then a separate nation, and the Byzantine Empire, an exchange which originally was based on trade. Very often, however, culture follows trade, and we know what the interaction of business and fine arts and ideas was in northern Italy and in the Renaissance in Europe as a whole. So when we speak of cultural exchange, whether in music or in anything else, we should be aware of the fact that we are dealing not with an innovation but with something which throughout history has more or less pervaded the relationship between nations—if not among all nations, then certainly among many of them, particularly those which have had an impact on the courses of art and intellect. I think it a safe generalization to state that those nations in the past most receptive to the ideas and to the arts of other nations, which they received on an "exchange" basis, were the ones which eventually built up a strong culture for themselves and consequently influenced their neighbors.

Here, however, I wish to dwell on cultural exchange, particularly in music as we have known it from about the turn of the century, with special reference to our own times. I am happy to treat this topic in my capacity as the executive director of Carnegie Hall, because if there is any institution in the United States which serves as the symbol of the values we seek in the international exchange of artists and ensembles it is Carnegie Hall. From its very inception Carnegie Hall was receptive to the artist, the ensemble, and the orchestra from abroad. Those who know the story of the origins of Carnegie Hall will recall that it opened in May 1891 and its guest of honor was Piotr Ilyitch Tchaikovsky, who came both to conduct and to hear some of his music. Since that time there have come to Carnegie Hall virtually every great soloist, ensemble, and orchestra, and leading personalities in the other arts and even in other fields we do not consider to be, strictly speaking, the arts. I think, for example, of the great pianist Ignace Paderewski, who, of course, did play on more than one occasion at Carnegie Hall, but it is interesting to note that he appeared at Carnegie Hall not only as a concert pianist but as an ardent and very eloquent spokesman for his native country, Poland, right after World War I.

When we say Carnegie Hall, we think too of its superb acoustics, which have enhanced the performances of many great orchestras over the years. These orchestras, of course, have been both from the United States and from other countries on tour in this country. It is odd to conceive of any great orchestra coming to this country which, at some point in its tour, does not perform at Carnegie Hall, and it is that appearance which becomes the acid test for the success of the tour as a whole, since the power of the New York critics in assessing the value of the orchestra is potent indeed. It is of some interest to note, as well, that many of the great American orchestras which have played and do play to this day at Carnegie Hall have been heard in countries both in Europe and in the Far East—notably among them the Philadelphia Orchestra under Eugene Ormandy; the Boston Symphony under its then-conductor Charles Munch and more recently under Erich Leinsdorf; the Cleveland Orchestra under George Szell; the Pittsburgh Symphony Orchestra, which not too long ago made a tour in the Middle East under William Steinberg.

There is more than a touch of drama in the recent story of Carnegie Hall as a building, as a cultural landmark. In 1959–60, the very real danger was faced of the hall being torn down to make room for a commercial structure. Those who followed the story with interest all over the world will recall that great efforts were made to save the hall and that these efforts succeeded. Thanks to a very determined group of citizens in New York City, prominent among them Isaac Stern, the violinist, but also including other artists and both civic and business leaders who were able not only to dramatize the need of keeping Carnegie Hall as a concert hall but also to convince the state government, and then through the state government the city government, of that need. Carnegie Hall, which until then had been under private ownership, was bought by the City of New York. The city entrusted its operations to a new group called the Carnegie Hall Corporation, not only to continue its great tradition as a concert hall but to develop new lines of activity which would enable Carnegie Hall to serve the growing cultural needs of the City of New York as well as of the country, and, I dare say, of the world at large. On July 1, 1960, Carnegie Hall entered its new existence. In addition to remaining the home of great concerts by solo artists, orchestras, and other ensembles, the hall through the corporation which operated it took more and more of an initiative in creating new program concepts, many of which have important international implications.

One of the most dramatic of these new program concepts is called the International Festival of Visiting Orchestras. This is an imposing series of concerts inaugurated during the season 1963–64 and continuing to this day. The purpose of this series is to bring together a number of great orchestras, both from the United States and from other countries, into one series with a carefully correlated repertoire so that people attending these concerts would, in the course of hearing them from week to week and month to month, be able to enjoy a generous sampling of the major orchestral literature as well as of the soloists appearing with the orchestras. And in the three seasons during which this International Festival of Visiting Orchestras has been operating at Carnegie Hall, we have had from other countries such great orchestras as the Royal Philharmonic from England, the Toronto Symphony, the Vienna Symphony, the London Symphony, the Warsaw Philharmonic, the Hague Philharmonic, and others.

The combination of orchestras from abroad and great orchestras from our own country, like those of Chicago, Philadelphia, Boston, Cleveland, Pittsburgh, and Minneapolis among others, has had, if I may use a sensational word, a "sensational" effect upon the concert-going public in New York City. Note that New York City has not had these great orchestras over the years or at least many of them, but never before had the attempt been made to schedule their concerts in such a way that there would be proper spacing of the dates so that people could subscribe to a series instead of attending only one or two of the concerts. To explain this in a little more detail: before we established the International Festival of Visiting Orchestras, when an orchestra came to New York, it took any date that seemed to be available and checked with no one to see whether the repertoire it intended to present at its concert or concerts would in any way duplicate the repertoire being given by other orchestras. The result was a kind of mild anarchy. I can remember seasons in which in a given week we would have as many as four or five concerts by orchestras from other cities and other countries. Then weeks would go by without any visiting orchestras. I also recall very vividly several years ago when the Brahms First Symphony was played by four different visiting orchestras within the span of ten days.

So what we have been able to accomplish, among other things, is the scheduling of concerts by these many visiting orchestras in such a way that we have a sensible continuity of dates right through the season. And by careful and sometimes extremely diplomatic negotiations with the various conductors, we avoid having Brahms's First or any symphony played to excess (I say this with no prejudice against the Brahms First, which I consider one of the truly remarkable creations of any composer). It might be amusing to note that last season five conductors wanted to do the Bartók Concerto for Orchestra. If Bartók could only realize how fashionable his Concerto for Orchestra has suddenly become, he would indulge in a sardonic smile over the posthumous success of the work. Well, we exercised a little diplomacy so as not to have too much of the one work, and we succeeded.

But an International Festival of Visiting Orchestras is more than a matter of mechanics. It is more than a matter of scheduling dates and reconciling repertoire and the like. It begins to build a certain pattern of concert-going among many people who instead of going occasionally to hear one or two of these visiting orchestras now hear them in succession over a number of months. And what is the result? Among other things, the public begins to hear how differently orchestras can sound; also that the same composer played by an orchestra, let us say, from Austria and played by an orchestra from Chicago sounds rather different, yet in both instances there is integrity of performance. It is not that one interpretation is right and another is wrong. Here we are dealing, of course, with a phenomenon in our musical life which, I think, adds another dimension to the whole question and to the whole value of cultural exchange. Up to a point, I think it is perfectly proper and rather exciting to say that a great orchestra from England has an English sound, that a great orchestra from Germany has a German sound, and so on, wherever the orchestra may come from. Note that I say a *great* orchestra, because when we are dealing with any traits in art, I think we should deal with only their greatest manifestations.

But the question of national traits in the sound of an orchestra can be stretched to absurd limits, and that is obviously not my intention here. I also know that to the audiences in New York hearing an orchestra from Vienna playing Mozart, for example, is an enormous revelation. At first there is, perhaps, a shock at hearing a Viennese orchestra playing Mozart in a different way than an American orchestra. The tempi are different; the whole approach seems to be different. But after this first shock, the audiences realize this must be as valid a Mozart, if perhaps not even a more valid Mozart than the one played by the American orchestra. Mozart, after all, came from the same country as the orchestra. And so we begin to compare interpretations, we begin to compare the special traits that seem to come out of the performances from different cities in this country and from different countries abroad. And as a result, we begin to realize that there is a much greater diversity, a greater variety, a broader spectrum in the whole experience of hearing music than if we were listening only to one orchestra, no matter how great, throughout the year because we had no opportunity of hearing another. This is one of the excitements and one of the special values of our International Festival of Visiting Orchestras.

It is said by some, and I will not take sides in this issue, that American orchestras tend to sound a little too juicy, tend to sound like an aggregate of virtuosi, tend to emphasize more the sensuous elements in orchestral sound and color, tend to emphasize a little unduly the technical accomplishments of the musicians of the orchestra. Be that as it may, we do know that the experience of hearing an American orchestra is a very exciting experience because of these qualities. It does not lessen the importance of the performance. It means another value; just as when we hear the great orchestras of Middle Europe, we hear more attention paid to the over-all line. It is perhaps a little slower; it is perhaps a little more reflective and to some ears a little more musical. It is another experience, and I am a pluralist when I approach any of the arts. I feel that there are many valid interpretations as long as you have both great ability and complete sincerity on the part of the interpreter. So that one of the values, one of the many values that we find in our cultural exchange (with stress here on orchestras) is to sense and savor the national traits of the country of the orchestra's origin through its music, through the way it plays, through the traditions of orchestral playing of that country and most particularly through the way a great work of a composer of that country is performed by the orchestra. There is a special thrill, for example, in hearing Dvořak played by a Czech orchestra. Dvořak does sound different with a Czech orchestra than with an orchestra of another country. Again I do not say it is better or worse; it is different and perhaps more "authentic" because of Dvořak's origin. The same would be true of a great French orchestra playing Debussy, a great English orchestra playing Vaughan Williams, and so on through the musical world.

Let me inject here a very human aspect of the value of cultural exchange. Again speaking largely of orchestras, I think back to the recent visits of such orchestras from abroad as the London Symphony, which in the span of eight days gave six concerts in New York City, five at Carnegie Hall and one at the United Nations. This is truly a remarkable number of concerts for a visiting orchestra to give in so short a span of time. To say that these concerts were executed magnificently is to say something which comes as no surprise to anyone who has heard the London Symphony Orchestra. What I should like to dwell on is the fact that we had in New York City for a period of over a week more than a hundred musicians from another country, the members of the London Symphony Orchestra, who sought out their counterparts in New York. A wonderful human quality emerged: to see a clarinetist, say, from the London Symphony sitting down with a clarinetist of the New York Philharmonic and comparing notes. The way we begin to respect others and, we trust, others begin to respect us is through the camaraderie of people in the same profession, respecting each other's ability and intentions, getting to know each other. And they are getting to know each other in the most effective fashion by traveling, thanks to the various plans of international cultural exchange in operation.

Since I did indicate earlier in the chapter that I wanted to use Carnegie Hall as a kind of image, symbol, or fulcrum of the values inherent in the whole concept of cultural exchange, particularly in music, let me go back for a moment and tell of some of the things that happen or are happening currently at Carnegie Hall which point up the excitement, the importance, and the variety of experiences through international exchange. I mentioned, of course, the International Festival of Visiting Orchestras, which last season alone had twenty-four concerts, but in addition we have been able to have a Beethoven Festival by the Berlin Philharmonic in a series of five concerts conducted by Herbert von Karajan. We also have had a Bach Festival by the Munich Bach Chorus and Orchestra under Dr. Karl Richter, in which major choral works were performed. In addition, we arranged with the BBC Orchestra for a festival of six concerts devoted entirely to music of the twentieth century with Antal Dorati and Pierre Boulez sharing honors as conductors. So here again is an indication of what happens in a city like New York. I have of course not given the entire picture but enough of a sampling to indicate how great an international arena New York is when it comes to orchestra music.

I want to indicate, too, in another area entirely of musical activity, how cultural exchange can operate. At Carnegie Hall we take great pride in several series of concerts which take place in our smaller hall, the Carnegie Recital Hall. They are held in the smaller hall because their appeal in numbers is more limited. These concerts are devoted to contemporary music, to very contemporary music. They are only presented after many rehearsals, by the very finest musicians available, so the performances are of top quality. New music often does not get all this attention. But what I really want to point out here is the great variety of music that is heard in such a series of concerts. The composers represented in these concerts are from many different countries of the world, so we hear some of the finer new music being composed in Italy, in France, England, Japan, or wherever it may be, including the United States, through concerts in Carnegie Recital Hall. These are conducted by Gunther Schuller, the well-known American composer, in his series "Twentieth-Century Innovations," or by the equally well-known composer Lukas Foss, who calls his series "Evenings for New Music." We are planning for another season to augment these concerts with a series of new quartet music, each program devoted to another country. There will be an evening, for example, of quartet music from Poland, the emphasis being on recent compositions. We want to hear what is going on in a country like Poland or the Netherlands or Japan or Italy or Israel, and we want to give each one of these countries its own evening. A very fine ensemble, the Philadelphia String Quartet, is already started on the repertory.

In another vein, in New York City, thanks in part to the presence of the United Nations and in part to the fact that New York increasingly has become a crossroads of the world, we have taken more and more of an active interest in so-called non-Western music and non-Western culture in general, in other words, the cultural manifestations which do not originate in Europe from the Renaissance to the nineteenth century—the cultures which have flourished in Africa, in Asia, throughout the world, which have taken their own course, which have developed in their own way into elaborate, exciting, and significant expressions of the human spirit. Again to indicate the values of international exchange, we are planning to offer still another series of concerts, each program of which will be devoted to another great school of non-Western music or the performing arts in general.

So much for some of the special things we are doing at Carnegie Hall, which points up the great international interest existing in a city like New York, an international interest that I know exists in equally great cities on other continents: cities like London, Paris, Berlin, Milan, Tokyo, Buenos Aires. It is very heartening to know that this international spirit that we sense in New York, which adds to the excitement of the cultural life of New York, is in large measure the very same quality and type of international experience that exists in these other cities. It establishes another kind of kinship—esthetically, artistically, spiritually, and humanly. I may also add that the very fact we have all these cross-currents of international art in a city like New York has stimulated our own domestic cultural life. It gives even further impetus to artists and to ensembles and to orchestras to develop their own audiences. One of the great examples at Carnegie Hall is the development of the American Symphony Orchestra under Leopold Stokowski; it is excellent.

I want to make special reference to the role of private foundations in this country, without which much of this activity could not have been established successfully. It is a well-known fact that, at least up to this moment, there is no real government subsidy of the arts in the United States, though we hope to see it begin soon. Certainly nothing exists here that is comparable to what happens in those countries which enjoy such subsidy.

Were it not for the fact that our foundations, both the very large ones and many of the smaller ones, have taken an interest in the arts, we would not have had the cultural development we now find in the United States. That the Ford Foundation and the Rockefeller Foundation, among the great ones, have been as active as they are is a well-known fact. I think it should also be known that we have smaller foundations which, in their own more modest way, do a great deal to encourage music making nationally and internationally. I mentioned the contemporary-music programs at Carnegie Hall. Were it not for the J. M. Kaplan Fund and the Martha Baird Rockefeller Fund for Music, we could not show what contemporary composers of many lands are creating in the way of new music.

Again using Carnegie Hall as a symbol—or, to use the other metaphor, as the fulcrum for what happens in the United States—of international implications in the arts and particularly in music, I want to speak of a very special function that Carnegie Hall fulfills which is not generally known because it does not require any broad publicity. Carnegie Hall, because of its great tradition, because of the varied activities in which it is involved, and because, shall we say, of its expert knowledge in so many areas of musical endeavor, is increasingly called upon not only in the United States but all over the world to give advice and certain forms of assistance to cultural projects in the making elsewhere. In recognition of this function, a number of years ago we created a sister organization called Carnegie Hall International, the function of which is specifically to be of assistance in every possible way in the creation of cultural projects anywhere in the world. By now Carnegie Hall International has been able to be of some assistance in at least a dozen countries in one way or another. Let me hasten to add that Carnegie Hall International is not rolling in funds. Our help, at least directly, cannot be in the form of money; but certainly the long experience of Carnegie Hall is available to the world.

There is one special outgrowth, however, of Carnegie Hall International which does require more publicity. It is one of the more exciting things that has happened in this country, again with an international aspect. This is the creation of a Jeunesses Musicales movement in the United States, a movement which began in Brussels and almost simultaneously in Paris in 1940, a movement which is directed to youth (defined by the International Federation of Jeunesses Musicales as those in the age group between fifteen and thirty), a movement which is dedicated to bringing the best of music to this age group as well as encouraging the more gifted members of this group to enjoy careers in the field of music. Since 1940 the movement has spread to some twenty-six countries which are full-fledged members of Jeunesses Musicales and about another fifteen countries which have Jeunesses Musicales movements in the making nationally. Jeunesses Musicales is a national movement in each country. Each country's organization controls its own destinies, but all countries are informally allied in the International Federation with headquarters in Brussels.

Ironically, the United States, despite all of its music making, was not a member of Jeunesses Musicales for reasons which space does not permit me to discuss here. But Carnegie Hall, through Carnegie Hall International, began a study of the Jeunesses Musicales movement several years ago. It was a study in depth and it came to the conclusion that, with certain modifications and certain amplifications, the Jeunesses Musicales movement could be of decided service to the musical life of the United States. As a result, not very long ago we were in a position to create "Carnegie Hall–Jeunesses Musicales," with headquarters in the Carnegie Hall building in New York City. But its effects are felt and will be increasingly felt throughout the United States, particularly on the campuses of colleges and universities where we are establishing local chapters of the Jeunesses Musicales movement. These local chapters will create a greater involvement, excitement, and significance in things musical among the students. This is in no way an attempt to substitute for the musical curriculum at a college or university but to augment the musical experience, the musical interest of students in general, whether or not they take studies in music at the college level.

There is another feature of Jeunesses Musicales which is of special interest. Over the years, it has been instrumental in fostering the careers of gifted younger artists, many of whom today rank among the well-established artists of international reputation. This has been accomplished through the exchange program, wherein, for example, France sends to the United States a fine cellist, in return for which the United States will send to France an equally fine pianist. Here in the United States, through our own Jeunesses Musicales movement, the French artist is able to go on tour and be heard, particularly by college audiences throughout the country, while the American artist going to France is heard at local chapters of the Jeunesses Musicales de France throughout that country. What happens with France also happens with Italy and Canada, and it can happen with members of other countries in the Jeunesses Musicales movement.

There is a value question I would like to bring up at this point. So far this chapter has been concerned more or less with the facts and in some small way the figures of what constitutes the international musical interest in America, with special reference to orchestras and to the role of Carnegie Hall. But let us ask ourselves, What are some of the values to us in the United States of having artists and orchestras coming from abroad, other than the value of listening to a glorious concert which, in itself, can be a sufficient justification of any such visit? Let us bear in mind that, perhaps more so than any other country, the United States has a population which, whether it be first generation or third generation, is of a multinational origin. The American population is made up of many people who, if not themselves born in another country, have parents or grandparents who were born in other countries; and the cultural instincts, if you will, the cultural biases, of the countries of origin were, in a more relaxed way, brought to this country by people who today are Americans just as other Americans. Now there is a collateral interest. Just as we are a nation in which the population in large measure is of multinational origin, so we must bear in mind that at least one positive consequence of the enormously tragic experience of World War II was that so many thousands upon thousands of young Americans for the first time went to other countries in military service. I am not going to say that they all flocked to the museums and art galleries and concert halls of the countries in which they were based, but as we sample their reactions we learn that a very appreciable number of them had their first encounter with great music and great art in countries other than their own and, when they returned home, they returned with a great desire, with an appetite to continue pursuing this interest. In a way, you might say that the cultural ferment taking place in this country can be attributed in part to the fact that so many young American men and women came back with an exposure to great culture, an exposure they might have had in this country if they had been able to get to the larger cities and if they had both the means and inducement to participate in the cultural life of those cities.

From my own firsthand experience, from the reports we read in the press, from the reports given to us by people who have been returning to this country from other countries, I know that many of the values I have indicated in artists and orchestras from abroad coming to the United States must be similarly felt by other countries when our American artists and orchestras visit them. That we have something to contribute which, in our own way, is as significant as what they have to contribute to us goes without saying; it is being demonstrated every day. That the excitement with which a great American orchestra is received is in some ways comparable, if not out of the same fabric, as the excitement with which a great European orchestra is heard in New York or in Chicago or Philadelphia or anywhere in this country I think also goes without saying. To me, one of the most heartening aspects of this converse situation is that we are living up to what at one time was the dream largely of philosophers and poets: the one-world concept, that a unified world can be established not so much through political effort, although I am not going to minimize the great work being done in that direction, but by the human spirit, particularly through the greatest manifestations of the human spirit, the arts. When an American pianist is heard in Moscow or a Russian violinist is heard in Buenos Aires, etc., you do not think of national differences, you are engulfed in an experience which is a truly universal one. It is an experience which levels differences, in which differences of nationality or politics are lost completely because they have no true relevance to the art experience.

We should encourage international exchange more and more, provided we are always exchanging great artists, great orchestras, the greatest manifestations of our arts, because the more we do the more we will discover that the differences between peoples are not so great as we thought, and that the similarities between peoples are based on those qualities, those values, which are all to the good, are constructive and which I trust would mean constructing a society for the future, a one-world society where we can all work together toward accomplishing the objectives we share in common. Idealistic, yes, but idealistic does not mean impossible, and if it is to be achieved, it will be achieved more through the arts than in any other way. It is curious that right here in America we can see this in a special context. I referred before to the great cultural ferment that has taken place here. By that I mean that, whereas culture was identified at one time principally with the large cities which had the major museums and the major symphony orchestras and the few major opera companies we possess, today we find what? Today we find important manifestations of cultural activity all over the country, in small towns as well as in large cities, but most particularly on the campuses of our colleges and universities. Our colleges have discovered that, in addition to the curriculum and the academic objectives of the schools, the general humanistic environment is of vast importance, that a student while he is studying and learning must live in an environment in which his deepest instincts, his humanistic instincts are stirred, not only through his course of study but through concert-going, through attending lectures, art exhibits, and the like. And this ferment we are experiencing is a marvelous bit of chemistry which accounts for the fact that in what otherwise would be an area isolated from the main roads and highways you can have great music being made and you can find a rather sophisticated audience. This was not true a generation ago, but it is becoming the rule today. Because of the ease of transportation here, the great artists and great orchestras from abroad are performing not only in the great cities, not only at Carnegie Hall, not only in New York or Chicago, Philadelphia or Washington, but throughout the country in places that I am sure most people in other countries never heard of; but they will hear of them because the visiting artists and orchestras upon their return will say that in the smaller American communities they had just as appreciative if not in some ways an even more appreciative audience than they had in the large cities. We can thank this internationalizing influence in the arts for the cultural ferment taking place in the United States, because that ferment in part is created by the tours of orchestras, ensembles, and artists from other countries.

15 FINANCIAL EVOLUTION OF THE ORCHESTRA

Samuel R. Rosenbaum

Except for their superior musical quality, there is really nothing unique about the half dozen or so great professional symphony orchestras that are usually mentioned when the subject of symphony orchestras in the United States is discussed. The symphony orchestras of Philadelphia, Boston, New York, and some other American cities are much like those of Berlin, Vienna, Paris, or London insofar as their general program structure and concert procedures are concerned. One can almost describe them as European symphony orchestras playing in the New World.

However, there is one aspect of their existence in which they differ markedly from their European exemplars. They are, by and large, supported by private, not by governmental, patronage and subsidy. This has effects possibly not realized by those who have not studied the subject.

Many, if not most, of the European symphony orchestras are cooperative enterprises governed by the players themselves; on the contrary, the American orchestras are, on the whole, governed by independent private nonprofit corporations administered or managed by representatives of the governing boards of citizens, and the players are employees of the organization. One consequence of this relationship is that the musical director of the orchestra is independent of the players, with an authority to require excellence of performance through the underlying power to hire and fire, subject, naturally, to the job-protection practices of local unions, but free of the often frustrating influence of internal relationships among the body of the players.

Without making invidious comparisons, or desiring to enter into the controversial area of qualitative judgments, it is probably true that most of the world's highly competent orchestra conductors agree, privately, that on the whole the top half-dozen American symphony orchestras are, for this reason, superior in musical proficiency and quality to their opposite numbers in European capitals. While many of the European symphony orchestras are run as cooperatives of the players, they are, however, composed of state employees who are engaged to play as the orchestra of the state-subsidized opera house in the city of their activity, with a modest guaranteed annual salary from the opera. Consequently, they become civil servants, with the protection of tenure, which tends to assure the players against the uncertainties of musical existence. While this is admirable from the human point of view, it is another factor in the relative diminution of driving force and ambition in European orchestras as compared with American ones. It is axiomatic that one cannot be both great and comfortable.

The whole structure of the economy of the American symphony orchestra has been made possible by another vital difference from its European counterparts. This is the provision in the United States Internal Revenue Code that permits a taxpayer to deduct from his taxable income 20 per cent for gifts or contributions he may make to such organizations as symphony orchestras. This provides an incentive for such gifts which does not exist in European countries, and largely explains why, in European countries, such entities as symphony orchestras are maintained by government and not by private subsidy. In the United States, it is estimated that the gross operating budgets of about twenty-five symphony orchestras usually described as the major orchestras run to about thirty million dollars a year; of this amount not over half is produced by such earnings as subscriptions and ticket sales, plus incidental revenue from recordings or broadcasts. The rest is contributed from private sources, mostly by private citizens and business corporations, contributions which are encouraged by the so-called gift deductibility from individual or corporate income subject to income tax. It is the risk of discouraging such gifts that gives pause to many promoters of our symphony orchestras when they are asked to support the growing movement for federal subsidy of the arts.

But apart from the obvious differences between American and European symphony orchestras in economics and management, there is another element in the symphony-orchestra life of America that is quite individual and unlike that which is prevalent in other countries. This is the existence of the so-called "community" or "civic" symphony orchestra, composed largely of music-loving amateur, nonprofessional performers.

Over twelve hundred such groups can be described as having sufficient continuity of existence and identity to justify their assuming the name of a symphony orchestra. Some have a history of many years of cooperative endeavor; each year during the last few decades their number has been increasing.

As of 1965, the year when the Report on Problems and Prospects of the Performing Arts was published by the Rockefeller Brothers Fund Panel, it is estimated that there were 60,000 persons playing regularly in symphony orchestras, of whom only about 7,200 are professionals, the rest being part-time players in 1,059 community orchestras and 228 college and university orchestras. In addition, there were 29 well-established "metropolitan" orchestras containing 2,200 players, of whom about 20 per cent were similarly amateurs. The total number of symphony orchestras had doubled since 1939.

This is a phenomenon of which few Europeans are even aware. It represents a movement in this country that is growing and acquiring increasing momentum. It deserves to be given some study. Let me mention some of the comments about it which are being made pro and con in music circles here.

Obviously and evidently the quality of performances by such groups is extremely varied. With some, according to the talent and experience of the participants, it is fair to good; with others, it is admittedly fair to poor. One very material factor is the ability and talent of the conductor. If he is a good teacher, with the love for his subject and his pupils which marks an inspired leader, the results will be better than if the conductor is merely an aspiring artisan who is seeking a change of occupation. A fair number of these orchestras are in the hands of gifted European refugees who arrived here too late in life to make the grade for fully professional positions in an occupation in which the competition is severe. Others provide a platform for gifted young graduates of conservatories who would otherwise have to wait indefinitely for an opportunity to conduct an orchestra. All in all, the general average of conducting is surprisingly high.

Nevertheless, carping critics (and they include some who are high in the ranks of the profession) are inclined to deprecate the activity of these wholly or largely amateur symphony orchestras on the ground that they cause both the players and the audience they succeed in attracting to be satisfied with inferior accomplishment. It is also argued that the inferior quality they present makes listeners disgusted with "live" music and relegates them to mechanical reproductions, such as phonograph records, where they can hear performances of superior quality. Counterwise, it is said that if audiences are satisfied with such second-rate performances it depreciates the taste of the listener and militates against the sacrifices necessary to sustain good performances by players of high quality who must be paid well for their efforts.

On the other hand, those who see merit in these amateur efforts point out that any such effort to make live music is better than being entirely satisfied with mechanical reproductions. Furthermore, it is pointed out that participation on any level is the best way for any music lover to understand the meaning of a good performance by a properly qualified professional, so that those who play in a community orchestra will make the best nucleus for an audience for the professional touring artist or orchestra.

It must be noted that the total audience for good music is increasing fairly rapidly in this country. While as yet it is estimated that the total number of different individuals who constitute the paying audience for the performing arts, including music, does not exceed one per cent of the entire population, it must nevertheless be recognized that the growing influence for good music exerted by the commercial music industries, such as phonograph records, radio, and television, is stimulating an ever-increasing public that accepts and even desires good music in that form. Optimists are convinced that this growing public for better records, radio, and television will gradually recruit growing numbers of paying audiences for good living music.

One statistic that is worth considering is the figure of sales of phonograph records that are commercially though unimaginatively labeled in the catalogue as "classical." Twenty years ago the gross volume of sales of the industry in this country was approximately $500 million, of which it was estimated that not over 15 per cent were of "classical" music. Today the gross is nearer to $700 million, of which it is estimated that possibly 25 per cent are in the "classical" catalogue, an increase from $7.5 million to $17.5 million a year, if these estimates are correct.

In any event, it is undeniable that at least an experience of good music is reaching many million more listeners through these mass media than ever before. The Recording Industries (Music Performance) Trust Funds, which I administer as trustee, receives requests for good chamber music and symphonic performances in many places so remote from the centers of population as to cause astonishment.

It is undoubtedly this contact with the literature of symphonic and chamber music that is responsible for the growing number of amateurs who wish to try their hand at actual live performance. Who can question the richness of satisfaction that comes with even imperfect participation as compared with being merely a passive listener of what we call in this country a "spectator sport"? It takes only a casual experience of playing or listening to live music in a concert hall to understand the truth of an observation I have often made when discussing this subject, that is, that "compared to the real thing, listening to music on phonograph records is like getting a kiss from your sweetheart over the telephone."

So what is happening is that an increasing number of these "community" symphony orchestras are springing up everywhere and nothing will discourage them. They reflect the irresistible urge of any normal human being to improve, even a little.

Who can doubt that, gradually and eventually, this movement will in the course of time create audiences for the professional performers, both in symphonic groups and otherwise, which will be qualified to appreciate good performance even without the circus trappings that too often are now used to attract customers, and will constitute the public support which will assure survival for good music?

Unfortunately it cannot be denied that, in the meantime, we have many more good performers than we have audiences for them, but the economic problems involved in the support of music and musicians are only of the same order as those which beset all the arts in this country, both creative and performing, in this generation. It is the existence of these problems which has stimulated the cry for federal subsidy as a solution, a remedy which still remains to be tested to convince many skeptics that it is the right one. This makes it germane to look for a moment at the manner in which performances of good music have so far been nourished in this country.

Usually a fairly small group of instrumental performers, generally nonprofessional, begins by gathering together for informal sessions of reading music in the ensemble literature, frequently inspired to do so by a local resident who is either a music teacher or a professional musician from Europe or from one of the centers of population. They usually get together once a week for music-reading sessions, until they think they have mastered a few works sufficiently to risk inviting an audience of sympathetic relatives and friends to listen to a concert.

Sometimes, in a larger town, this process begins with the arrival of a musician who has long aspired to be a conductor and who eggs on a group of pupils, friends, or music lovers generally to establish a local orchestra. Probably it is unjust to repeat it, but there is the popular anecdote that goes: If a musician in Europe has a love affair with a wealthy lady, the result is an addition to the population, whereas in America the result is more apt to be a new symphony orchestra.

This is because it is well known that for a symphony orchestra to have good quality, it must have at least a nucleus of professional or trained musicians in it; and to hold the interest of these, it is desirable, if not essential, that they be compensated for their services. A local symphony can exist in fair health with wholly volunteer services in the management but not in the performing personnel.

Many of the part-time orchestras give as many as four public concerts a season, for which rehearsals take place every week during the season. Some have grown into more strongly established institutions that venture a somewhat longer schedule during the season. After a fair start, the community orchestras muster enough financial support to employ a few more professional or union players, and then a few more, until, in some cases, the orchestra has more professional than amateur player-members; and, finally, the last stage, and the most costly, is to reach the point where the community or the supporters are not satisfied with anything but the best they can afford, and convert the operation into a wholly professional orchestra. This has been the history of most of the symphony orchestras, some thirty or forty in number, which are now wholly professional in playing membership.

As a concert hall with not over two thousand seats is about the limit for satisfactory acoustics in most cities (and there is a fairly low limit to the number of concerts which an orchestra can play while maintaining high professional quality, or, indeed, to the number of concerts which a community will attend), it becomes apparent that in order to hold the personnel of well-paid (or, better to say, even modestly paid) performers, and to hold the admission prices down to a level within the reach of the families in middle economic brackets, it is necessary to solicit cash benefactions from those families in the community who may be better off than the average.

This has been the uniform experience of all of us who endeavor to maintain a good symphony orchestra in any American community. The five or six leading orchestras in the country, though some of them have gathered fairly substantial invested endowment funds, all are under the necessity of conducting annual fund-raising drives in which they must collect at least several hundred thousand dollars each in order to meet expenses.

The interesting fact is that they succeed. Although practically every one of the great symphony orchestras faces the risk of failure in this annual effort, and although, from time to time, the board of directors lose heart and threaten to discontinue, the tenure of employment in the symphony world has remained more unbroken and more secure than in almost any other area of the craft. At one time, theater-pit orchestras bade fair to draw players away from underpaid symphony jobs; today there is hardly a single theater with a pit orchestra. In a later decade, the big name bands in the dance-band field began to attract players from the symphony field. Today the name bands are only a memory. Still later, the radio studios drew good players away from the symphonies, many of whom moved to California to share the golden flood there. Today the radio orchestras are almost a thing of the past. Yet there are more jobs in the symphony world today than ever before. True, they are not all handsomely paid. It is lamentable that in many of the orchestras, the season is not more than twenty to thirty weeks, and the pay ranges down to under one hundred dollars a week, but at least it provides a basis on which a musician can establish a small business by teaching and playing odd jobs as well. Finally, through the pressure properly exerted on the concert-going public and the managing orchestra boards by unrelenting union representations and demands, we are now at last entering upon an era in which guaranteed year-round employment is being obtained by the players in the few top orchestras, with the hope that, slowly and gradually, this accomplishment will set the example for all.

In the leading orchestras—Philadelphia, New York, and Boston —the minimum player now has a contract which assures him of pay for fifty-two weeks a year, including four weeks of paid vacation, at a gross pay of at least $12,000 per annum, and this example is already being adduced as a clinching argument in several other great cities.

In no other country in the world is there such an outpouring of private means for the support of music. It is desirable that this phenomenon be known and understood in quarters where America is often portrayed as solely materialistic and interested only in making money. It is precisely because of the money-making proclivities of our population that a level of prosperity has been achieved which makes it possible to gather benefactions for the support of culture in such munificent degree.

At least, so far as gifts from private citizens are concerned, there is no selfish motive in such contributions for the support of symphony orchestras. They are given for much the same motives that in other countries animate gifts made to the church, that is, to help the less well situated to enjoy the blessings of great music and to improve the cultural tone of the community as a whole. There may be some element of snob appeal at times, but certainly in this form it can only be approved and encouraged rather than have it take the form of conspicuous spending for horses, jewels, palaces, and other outward indices of wealth.

In recent years, a new source of contributions for the arts, including music, has become manifest—donations from corporate treasuries. The Revenue Code also encourages such gifts by permitting a deduction of 5 per cent of net taxable income for such contributions. More and more, the corporation executive is recognizing that the modern American concept of capitalism acknowledges an obligation to the community in general as well as merely to the stockholder. It would be obvious if the motivation for a contribution from a corporation were merely for what is called public relations, that is, in a sense to purchase good will in a given community, or, on the other hand, if the expenditure were merely a form of advertising either of the product or of the institution and the cost justified as an investment in distribution or in painting the corporate image.

However, the most enlightened managements now go beyond such concepts, though the broader view does not exclude them. A striking example is that of the Standard Oil Company of New Jersey and its Latin-American affiliates. In 1965 this congeries of business corporations, with large interests in every Latin-American country, made generous and substantial contributions toward the cost of traveling art exhibitions showing the accomplishments of Latin-American painters and toward the cost of the Inter-American Music Festival held in Washington, D.C., without any commercial connections or exploitation other than the mere mention of its name. This example has already inspired similar attitudes in a small number of other large commercial organizations.

However, locally all over the United States, a growing number of corporations are making contributions to charitable and cultural causes. In fact, many of us who concern ourselves with the maintenance of cultural organizations in the arts, both performing and creative, believe that the major support for them in coming decades will be from this source, and that, on the whole, this might be preferable to the risk of mediocrity that might accompany the influence of federal subsidy. However, this is new territory and it remains to be seen how it will be tilled.

Certainly it is difficult to envision the manner in which governmental subsidy can be intelligently applied to the process of slow growth which is spreading the community-symphony idea all across the continent and causing the gradual transformation of the community symphony into first a partly professional and ultimately a wholly professional organization. The strength of the movement as it exists today, with all the headaches and heartaches that it is heir to, lies in the very fact that it has roots in the soil, that it responds to a natural not an artificial demand, and that it results from the gradual enlightenment of the whole population.

When one compares the general level of average public taste in this country with what it was before World War II, and then with what it was before World War I, one can only agree that it is immeasurably higher and better informed than before, and is improving steadily through the influence of two irresistible forces: the mass media of communication and the steady increase in the number of colleges and universities with the accompanying improvement in the general character of universal education.

There are, of course, many evidences and outbursts of vulgarity and vitality which are inevitable in a country with only two centuries of top-level cultivation behind it. However, it cannot be denied that the general level of taste and cultivation is high and rising every year. It is this criterion which will be applied by the Muse of History, rather than comparison of a few brilliant talents at the top.

16 THE STATUS OF THE COMPOSER

William Schuman and Samuel R. Rosenbaum

SAMUEL R. ROSENBAUM: *We would like to discuss the position of the American composer of serious concert music today. I know you have many thoughts on the subject. What we are particularly interested to learn is, What are your views about his status, his prospects, the way that the public receives him, and what are the possibilities for him to do the creative work for which the Lord gave him his talents?*

WILLIAM SCHUMAN: I must say that the most difficult title to carry in the world in which we live is that of "composer," because it is the one that is least understood and perhaps least appreciated. But of course the person in any society who writes serious concert music is obviously creating a product that rarely in the entire history of the arts has been an object of wide popular consumption.

The questions you pose are fascinating, but they are extraordinarily broad. Let me ask you first to rephrase your question. Make it a little more specific. Then I might bring some of the areas into sharper focus.

MR. ROSENBAUM: *Good. Let us start by asking this question: How does an American composer of serious music make a living?*

MR. SCHUMAN: You can divide that into two parts immediately. I would say that part of his income comes directly from the writing of music and part comes from other activities that are corollary or tangential. Here again we must make a further differentiation. If you speak of the top eight or ten composers in this country, I think you can say without fear of contradiction that they earn a satisfactory living just from writing music. But if you take the majority of composers in this country, that is to say those who have high professional attainment (and we could name upward of a hundred, not just taking the stars but very capable composers), I think you will find that, in general, only a small percentage of their income comes directly from writing music. As to the other activities in which they engage, we all know that they are principally in the teaching profession. In truth, this has been a great boon to our universities and conservatories. Others work in editorial capacities, or as instrumentalists, or as conductors, performers, or lecturers. For the most part, they earn their living in the teaching profession, not from composition itself.

MR. ROSENBAUM: *Would you say, however, that, on the whole, there is more consideration now being given to the needs of the composer by various organizations, such as foundations, universities, institutions, both industrial and otherwise in this country, than was the custom in the past?*

MR. SCHUMAN: I myself would be chary about comparing what we do in this country with customs of the past, except to say that one of the things we like to emphasize in general is youth. A great deal is done for the young composer. It is virtually impossible for a young composer of profile to escape notice. I use the word "profile" advisedly. If he does not have a distinguished profile, he is not a composer; he is merely someone trained in the techniques of musical expression or musical projections. Unless he has a profile that is recognizable, he would not be honored as a composer; but I would say for one who is young, it would be almost impossible for him not to be recognized if he has a distinguished personality.

There are in this country not only many foundations that give help through grants, but there are composers who work on committees to help other composers. There is the National Institute of Arts and Letters, for example. There are programs by our performing rights organizations that attempt to help young composers with grants. I would say, on the whole, that the position for the young composer is excellent.

MR. ROSENBAUM: *One of the great difficulties that I have observed is the need for what I have heard described as a society for second performances. Would you say that the same thing is true about the composer who is not actually a fledgling, is established as a craftsman but yet needs support for the dissemination of his product?*

MR. SCHUMAN: I would rather look at it this way: if you take the standard composers of contemporary music in this country, that is, the leading six or eight, you will find that in their catalogues of works there will always be several which will be widely performed. These works are usually those that are fairly easy to perform and more readily accessible to public appreciation. However, even the most performed among us will find that the more difficult works we write are not as often performed. It is perfectly true that even after you have an established reputation, if the work proves too difficult, you know that other performances will follow less frequently. Conductors like the glamour of the première. It gives them a page in the history book, but they are a little chary of repeat performances if the public does not accept the work.

MR. ROSENBAUM: *Not long ago, I had occasion to visit friends of mine who are active in concert promotion in cities like London, Paris, Vienna, and Berlin. They all tell me that the audiences in those musical centers are most conservative in their tastes, and that it is extremely difficult to persuade conductors to program contemporary works either from their own country or other countries. Do you find, on the whole, that there is as much or more or less receptivity on the part of conductors in this country for contemporary concert compositions by our composers?*

MR. SCHUMAN: I think that the audiences in metropolitan centers in the United States tend to be more liberal. They have had a broader experience. However, if you go into the smaller communities, you very often find less sophisticated audiences. Of course, the most exciting audiences are the university audiences that are looking for new experiences. They are not afraid; they do not shy away from new sounds.

I have found, in general, that the major orchestras in Europe cannot be really fairly isolated and classified as a group. Some of them are extraordinarily conservative. Some cities are extremely conservative—Paris and London, for example—while other centers in Europe are much more liberal. I do not think experimentation and the production of works of a controversial nature is to be expected of large establishments in any human endeavor. To this, music is no exception.

MR. ROSENBAUM: *Is it not true that our major symphony orchestras have such gigantic budgets that it is very difficult for them to experiment?*

MR. SCHUMAN: I think this is true. However, I have a rather strong conviction on this subject, as you would expect. It seems to me that if you forget the symphony orchestras for a moment and go to publishing houses, the great publishing houses of the past have always accepted an obligation to publish a certain amount of new music whether or not it made its way commercially. Actually this is really enlightened self-interest. In the long run, by promoting a Debussy during the early days of his career when he was not very successful, the publisher who stayed with him made out very well. There is only one major recording company that is not afraid to record new music. Of the major publishing houses, only a few publish new music.

When you come to the symphony orchestras, it seems to me

what is lacking is a conviction on the part of the board of directors. Whether the music is accepted or not, it is part of their responsibility to the art of music to produce it. If they were living in the time of Beethoven, they would not be performing Beethoven any more than they do their contemporaries today. I think when we make these generalities, however, we tend to overlook the large quantity of contemporary music that actually is played by the orchestras in the United States. A great deal is played, but it is still relatively an infinitesimal amount.

If I may return to your opening question, the fact that so little music is played, in terms of percentages, by our symphony orchestras points up the economic dilemma of the composer. I remember my first performance in Philadelphia—my Fourth Symphony—more than twenty years ago. I remember going down there for rehearsals and coming back to my teaching job in New York. I did not make enough royalties from that performance to cover the expenses of going to and from Philadelphia. My performances then were few and far between. The copyist of your music often makes more money than you do composing it.

MR. ROSENBAUM: *Do you think that the cost and expenses which are involved in preparing a new composition for performance militate to put difficulties in the way of the composer—I mean such expenses as the payment to the musicians who must perform even an experimental work, and the costs of copying and extraction of parts? Is this an important element in the life of a composer?*

MR. SCHUMAN: It is very important, but I am a hopeless romantic in answering this question. I think if the material is really exciting, the music will get produced. One can always look for excuses. I would prefer to look inward.

MR. ROSENBAUM: *You do not have to explain that you are an incurable romantic optimist, because if you were not you would not be following the profession of a composer. There is a great deal of talk in the air these days, Bill, about govern-*

ment support for music and for musicians and the possibility for composers. Do you have any views as to whether or not, as conditions are in this country as compared with some others, it would be wise or helpful or desirable for some government agency to have funds to hand out for composers?

MR. SCHUMAN: When the question of government subsidy is presented, it is always presented as though it were a theoretical issue. To me it is not a theoretical issue because in many forms it already exists. Without for a moment comparing this country with other countries, notably European countries, I think I would like to answer this way: I believe that in this country we are developing what I would like to think of as a twentieth-century American solution to some of the problems of music and other performing arts. I do not think that we have all the answers, but I think we have learned that we must tap all sources of support. We believe in the initiative of the individual patron as the basic source of what we are doing because in that way there are no extrinsic controls imposed. We also count very heavily on the philanthropy of private foundations, which are virtually unknown in Europe. In this country it is our government's way of supporting the arts. I would like to explain that for a moment. The United States government permits any citizen to deduct from his taxable income up to 20 per cent of his net earnings to support good works for charitable purposes, including cultural projects. In that way, if a man is heavily taxed in a 50-per-cent bracket and gives a hundred dollars to a symphony orchestra, it only costs him fifty dollars, as the government is paying the other fifty. This is one of the great devices we have in this country of government support. So when people ask me: "When will government support come?" I answer: "We have it now."

There will also be increased direct government support. The government is subsidizing the sending of artists abroad to show that this country cares very deeply about spiritual and cultural values. There also are arts councils in some twenty-odd states. We are getting recognition for the arts at the highest level, which we have not previously had. I believe in the years immediately ahead, if we can establish a reasonable basis for peace in the world, and that is basic to everything we are talking about, we will see a flowering in the support of the arts in this country that will tap all the sources I have indicated and will include corporate giving as well.

MR. ROSENBAUM: *Would you agree with me that, on the whole, the general level of public taste of this country has risen immeasurably in the last half-century, thereby creating an ever-increasing demand from the general public for the best in the product of the arts, including music and composition?*

MR. SCHUMAN: I could not agree with you more. When I read articles which say that there are too many performing musicians, that we do not have the audience for them, I say this is absolutely not a case of overproduction of musicians, it is a case of under-consumption of the product. Our audiences have grown immeasurably, not only in sophistication, which you point out, but also in numbers. But the numbers are still relatively infinitesimal in terms of the percentages of the population.

Not long ago, the New York Philharmonic gave three concerts in Central Park, and, as you probably have heard, for the first one there was an audience of seventy thousand people. Everybody said that was just a strange coincidence, but at the next one there were seventy-three thousand people; when they played a concert on Staten Island, where the population I gather is something in the neighborhood of two hundred fifty thousand, about twenty-five thousand people attended. If we had 10 per cent of our population in New York City (which would be roughly a million people) coming to the Philharmonic, we would have to build six Lincoln Centers in New York to accommodate them.

We have not begun to spread the joys of the performing arts

to all our people, because so many of our people do not know they are available to them, either in economic terms or in terms of their seeing themselves in such surroundings.

MR. ROSENBAUM: *Certainly that coincides with my observation. Would you also agree that, to a certain extent, the increase in the public acceptance of the best in the production of the arts, including music, is due to the influence of the media of mass communications?*

MR. SCHUMAN: This is always said, and it is said so often and with such assurance that I am sure there must be a great truth in it. My own observation is that in the field, say, of recording, which is one of the great methods, of course, for promoting the dissemination of music, it is my observation (though I cannot document this, so I put it forth as an observation for whatever it is worth) that there are two separate worlds. I think the collector of phonograph records is not frequently, curiously enough, the person who goes to concerts, and the person who goes to concerts is not necessarily the record collector. We seem to have developed separate publics. The larger is that of the phonograph listener. He hears music in reproduction which, however excellent, can never, never equal the real thing. It is like a magnificent painting of El Greco reproduced in black and white.

MR. ROSENBAUM: *The expression I use is: It is like getting a kiss from your sweetheart over the telephone. Bill, many of my friends who admire the Russian style of supporting the arts banter with me over the relatively more secure position, as they describe it, of the composer in Russia. In the Soviet economy the composer is provided with a villa, or* dacha, *and an apartment, which is rather rare; and he can work and compose as he chooses, they say. Do you feel that, on the whole, the ills that the composer is heir to in this country are worth the comparative freedom he enjoys?*

MR. SCHUMAN: I most certainly do. Within the last seven or eight years, a group of distinguished Russian composers headed by Dmitri Shostakovitch, visited this country, including Dmitri Kabelevsky and Tikhon Khrennikov, and several others whose names do not come to mind at the moment. I had the privilege of receiving these composers when president of the Juilliard School of Music. I showed them through our library and I think they were astonished by the open shelves where anyone could come in and pick up any piece of music, including, of course, a couple of examples of their own. They found some programs there in which was included some rather extreme modern music. They asked me whether I admired this music. I inquired: "You mean me, personally?" They replied: "Personally." I said: "No." "You do not," they said, "but yet you are the head of the school and you are programing it. Why?" I tried to explain to them that we would not really have been an intellectually honest institution if we had not introduced our students to all the principal artistic developments of the present-day world as well as of the past. A little later in the week we met them again with some of our own composers. Five of us were talking with them, and we got on the subject of conformity. We agreed, on our side, that we would all like to be honored in our own countries in the economic ways they were but that we preferred to have the lack of conformity that we enjoyed rather than having to rationalize the kind of music we write. They considered control to be freedom, even to the extent of having every student in the conservatory studying exactly the same pieces in every major city of the Soviet Union at the same time. I asked one of them what happens if you have a difference in the talent of the student and the talent of the teacher and he answered: "There you put the finger on a problem." But the point is that they regard as bondage the conditions we regard as freedom.

Perhaps I have stated this in terms that are much too broad. An artist is an artist wherever you find him, and splendid artists of a totalitarian world are no less splendid because they are shackled. But if you would ask me if I would trade economic security for dictatorship of any kind, esthetic or political or any other, my answer would be an absolute no, without any question whatsoever.

MR. ROSENBAUM: *Previously, Bill, you said that you estimated there might be a hundred composing talents in this country worthy of recognition. Would you say that is a large or small number in view of the number of musicians we have?*

MR. SCHUMAN: I feel that in terms of the past we have no way of knowing really how many wonderful composers existed at the time of Beethoven. We know that Ludwig Spohr was more popular then. He was more performed than Beethoven, but now he is mostly a history-book character. Whether there were many composers whose works were entitled to performance by major orchestras or opera companies then, I do not know. I do know, however, that history produces very few fine composers at any one time. It is interesting that history has always produced very few composers of stature compared to the numbers of authors and painters, let us say. I think one reason for this is that it takes at least twelve to fifteen years of very hard and arduous study before a person can become even a poor composer. So I would say that what we have in the United States is an astonishing technical proficiency on the part of many composers. I attribute this to the fact that so many composers of the last two generations have been teaching in schools and spreading the gospel. You can hardly name any major American city without being able to point to several excellent composers in it. I think this is a wonderful development, and it fills me with great hope for the future.

MR. ROSENBAUM: *Would you say on the whole the teaching of music in the schools and conservatories of this country is rising to higher levels of excellence?*

MR. SCHUMAN: I would like to say that, but I cannot. I think that public-school music, in spite of fine efforts being made by some very distinguished leaders, is still a very gray area, with wonderful exceptions. For example, I know of several large cities which have extraordinary music programs. On the other hand, other school systems, including those of some major cities, leave a great deal to be desired. High-school bands range from the mediocre to the superb. Some are absolutely breathtaking. Very few professional bands in the world can touch them.

Then take the development of the orchestras in the United States; I think all my friends from Europe agree that there are no orchestras in the world superior to those found in so many cities, large and small, in the United States.

MR. ROSENBAUM: *Do you think that the general public should be called upon and recruited more than it is to support composers?*

MR. SCHUMAN: I think the general public should do much more in the way of supporting the art of music; and institutions in music, in turn, should do more to support the creative artist. I believe that if there were more men on boards of directors who understood this, and if leading artists would have more conviction, they would agree that it is their job to lead the laity. The laity cannot be expected to know the problems in so complex a field. I think the thing to do is support the established institutions, to help create new ones, and see they have a philosophy which truly reflects the democratic spirit of the United States. It is better that support for the arts be widespread always, however, with the understanding that excellence must be the prime and sole criterion.

MR. ROSENBAUM: *Well, Bill, you have given us a prescription that is a trumpet call to action and we are very grateful to you for enlightening us in this way about the present and the future. One more aspect of the life of the composer I would like to ask you about is this: Do you think that good work is being done by institutions, like the MacDowell Colony or the Huntington Hartford efforts of recent memory, to encourage worthwhile composition?*

MR. SCHUMAN: Yes, time in the beautiful hills of New Hampshire to really work under undisturbed conditions is, of course, a boon to many artists, and I think it is very important.

MR. ROSENBAUM: *Do you think it is necessary for a creative personality like a composer to have complete rest and isolation? I think you have never had that in your entire career.*

MR. SCHUMAN: I believe this is entirely a matter of temperament. I mean I personally would go out of my mind if I had all my time to write music and my publisher would go broke. I feel I would like to function in a public life as well as in a private life. Many other composers show the same tendency. My work used to be teaching, now it is administrative.

MR. ROSENBAUM: *Do you think it is characteristically an American phenomenon that so large a number of commissions for compositions are available, such as from the Koussevitzky Foundation, the Louisville Commissions, or the Rockefeller Foundation, and others?*

MR. SCHUMAN: No composer likes anything better than a commission. In the first place, it shows him that someone wants the work, someone is willing to pay for the work, and the performance is all set for the work, so that you are composing for a specific need. I think the number of commissions we have is extraordinary and is a most satisfying development.

MR. ROSENBAUM: *Do you think, on the whole, that the commercial music publishers are equally interested in stimulating composition?*

MR. SCHUMAN: When you use the word "commercial" it means the sole object is to make money. I think that any commercial publisher is interested in commissioning any work that will enhance his earning power. I do not say this critically; I am simply describing it.

MR. ROSENBAUM: *Many of us who have been commissioning works from composers find that the results, on the whole, are not really as satisfactory as if a composer feels the urge to write something that expresses something he wants to say. How do you feel?*

MR. SCHUMAN: I do not think this is the experience by and large with the established composers. After all, Bartók wrote his most popular work, the Concerto for Orchestra, on commission from the Koussevitzky Foundation you just mentioned. About two years ago the Library of Congress had an entire festival of commissioned works which seemed to me to be all excellent examples of the work of the composers commissioned.

MR. ROSENBAUM: *Bill, I gather that, on the whole, you feel rather optimistic about the future of compositions and composers in this country. Is this correct?*

MR. SCHUMAN: Yes, I do, indeed.

17 OUTLOOK

Paul Hume

An immensely vital part of the musical development of the United States can be traced by studying the growth of its symphony orchestras. The oldest of these is the New York Philharmonic, whose year of birth is the same as that of the Vienna Philharmonic, 1842. In the century and a quarter that has intervened since the founding of the New York Philharmonic, there has been a steady, if sometimes slow and at other times astonishingly rapid, proliferation of symphony orchestras in this country, to the point where today, according to the lists of the American Symphony Orchestra League—which is a kind of central clearinghouse in all matters orchestral in this country—there are now fifty-eight orchestras of the first and second rank. In order that we may understand the basis on which this particular rank is assigned, let me say that it is determined by economics according to the League's classifications: all orchestras which engage their players on a seasonal contract, and which have annual budgets of not less than $250,000, are called "major," while orchestras which have annual budgets between $100,000 and $250,000 are classified as "metropolitan." Thus these designations are wholly economic in basis, and not derived at all from artistic measures.

Immediately we have raised, either explicitly or implicitly, certain vital questions that surround any discussion of symphony orchestras in our country today. We have said "orchestras which engage their players on a seasonal contract." Notice that I did not say, "on a year-round contract," or even anything like "on a contract of not less than, say, twenty-eight weeks, or thirty-six, or forty-two." And notice that the metropolitan orchestras are so designated purely on the basis of their budgets, with no consideration of contract whatsoever.

Clearly the condition of our symphony orchestras is totally intertwined with problems of economics. Yet the cultural force of these orchestras is an immeasurable factor in our national life today, and must be outlined at this point before we proceed any further. In the years when it was habitual for us who live in the United States to point to Europe as a guide and model in the realms of musical development, we were accustomed to saying: "But see how every European city and often smaller community has its own opera house." And we would speak of Baden-Baden and Parma and enviously of Dresden and Zagreb, and we would think of the large number of Americans who had gone to Europe to study opera because their own country would not or could not give them a place to sing in opera houses of our own.

Then, after a while, we began to realize that, if we lacked opera houses and opera seasons in the United States, we had something which Europe did not have: a symphony orchestra in Milwaukee, and one in Houston, another in New Orleans, and still others in Buffalo and Kansas City and St. Louis and Denver and Seattle. And it came to pass several years ago that a famous Viennese conductor toured this country with the Vienna Philharmonic. When they came to a smaller city, he played the most familiar works of Beethoven, Schubert, and Richard Strauss. And after the concert, a man from the audience came back to see him and asked him: *"Aber, lieber Meister, warum haben Sie nicht eine Sinfonie von Bruckner für uns gespielt?"* And the conductor said later that he was astonished to find in this medium-sized city in the middle of the United States someone who could discuss the Fourth Symphony of Bruckner in detail. Yet this kind of acquaintance with a large symphonic repertoire is by no means uncommon, thanks to the spread of symphony orchestras across the country, though I must add that the coming of the long-playing phonograph record has also had a large part in our musical knowledge.

Yet, despite the number of orchestras in the United States today—and there are eighty-six in the two principal categories I have mentioned—we cannot claim a flourishing existence for many of these organizations. Indeed, for those in the "metropolitan" category, of which there are, as of January 1967, fifty, the history of each has been an unending struggle for existence, while those which are called "major," of which there are twenty-six, have, with few exceptions, had precisely the same struggle. We are not now speaking *artistically;* that is a situation which has varied directly with the talents of the various conductors who have led each orchestra. By general agreement, the *finest* orchestras of the United States today are those of Boston, New York, Philadelphia, Cleveland, and Chicago. We are now speaking of absolute technical competence, the quality of tone, the high artistic standards of each individual player, and the general musicianly level of the conductors of these orchestras. Close behind these five stand the orchestras of Pittsburgh, Los Angeles, Detroit, and Minneapolis. Incidentally, I must state here, simply for the record and as a matter of simple fact which I shall not enlarge upon, with one single exception, that not one of the conductors of those nine orchestras is a native-born American. They came from Austria, Hungary, France, Germany, India, Sweden, and Poland. Leonard Bernstein, at the head of the New York Philharmonic, is the only native American conductor in that group.

Now the importance of our symphony orchestras to our national cultural development is something that has long been widely acknowledged. As for the significance of that cultural development as a whole, it was the late President John F. Kennedy who wrote, on June 10, 1963: "I have long believed . . . that the quality of America's cultural life is an element of immense importance in the scales by which our worth will ultimately be weighed." * Later in the same letter, he continued: "Government surely has a significant part to play in helping establish the conditions under which art can flourish—in encouraging the arts as it encourages science and learning."

It was President and Mrs. Kennedy who played a highly significant part in greatly heightening official encouragement of the arts and artists, while their personal interest in the arts also had a vital place in increasing the assistance which has come to the arts in most dramatic form in past months.

What was the nature of the economic struggle in which our orchestras were so deeply and for much of their lifetimes engaged? And why was the government's official encouragement of the arts needed in the way of which President Kennedy spoke? Finally, what new and unprecedented measures did private assistance take, simultaneously with and parallel to the historic action set in motion by President Kennedy and carried forward by President Johnson? These questions are our chief concern here, and their answers come from the period of a single month, during which the history and progress of symphony orchestras in the United States changed abruptly at the most critical juncture in their history.

The economic problems of almost every orchestra in this country were the same, as August Heckscher, who was Special Consultant for the Arts to President Kennedy, wrote in his statement on "The Arts and the National Government" † in the summer of 1963: "Despite favorable social and political tendencies, the condition of the professional arts in the United States is not in all regards satisfactory. The very demands which changing public tastes have made upon established artistic institutions have

* Letter from President Kennedy to August Heckscher, June 10, 1963. Printed in Senate Document No. 28, 88th Congress, 1st Session.
† "The Arts and the National Government," by August Heckscher. Printed in Senate Document No. 28, 88th Congress, 1st Session.

strained the financial resources available to them. Older forms of patronage have not in all cases been adequately replaced . . . Often, inadvertently, government has imposed obstacles to the growth of the arts and to the well-being of the individual artist."

Among the economic changes that came specifically to symphony orchestras were those created by change in the tax structure and the rise in every kind of cost to management, such as printing bills, union musicians' wage demands, rents and artists' fees, while the prices of tickets very quickly reached a ceiling beyond which it was completely unreasonable to raise them. Yet when we speak of musicians' salaries, we touch on one of the sorriest aspects of the entire situation. For example, in the year 1964, even among the *leading orchestras,* the average contract salary was only slightly over $5,000. Only four orchestras offered their players full-year contracts, and most symphonies offered thirty weeks or less. Furthermore, the low income possible for even the finest orchestral players tends to discourage young people from the long and expensive years of training necessary for symphonic careers, which thus endangers the future quality of our orchestras. Strikes among our leading orchestras broke out in recent years in such privileged symphonic cities as Philadelphia, Chicago, New York, and Washington, while St. Louis, where the struggle has been especially difficult, canceled its entire 1965–66 season and was only able to restore it in part after heroic, last-minute measures had been taken.

In the United States, there has been no such thing as federal-government subsidy of the arts in any direct form, and almost none in any indirect form that amounted to any significant sum. Nor have the individual states or cities moved into this area in the absence of any lead from the central federal government, and this in spite of the examples of every other country in any way oriented to Western musical civilization where government assistance to the arts has been offered over a period of years that reach from little more than a decade to centuries. In the United

States, while every one of our presidents has paid lip service to the arts, it is only recently that the power of the Presidential office has been put firmly behind any such move. And, while we talk a great game about being a cultured nation, or even a musical one, there is a vast amount of opposition, some of it quite well reasoned, to any kind of subsidy. Yet the facts are clear and are borne out by the boards of trustees of several hundred of our symphonies: that, whereas ten years ago those trustees were 90 per cent opposed to any form of subsidy, in 1965 they voted by precisely the opposite number, *90 per cent in favor* of such aid. For without it, it is now apparent that some of our leading orchestras will be unable to continue.

Musicians are no longer willing to spend many years in arduous and costly studies, only to be hired for little more than half of the year in music, so that the rest of the time, in order to feed themselves and their families, they must work at repairing automobiles, selling houses, driving milk wagons, and other kinds of incompatible jobs.

With this fact as history and these problems squarely on our doorsteps, it was nothing less than staggering, in a quite wonderful way, to see passed late in September 1965 the National Foundation on the Arts and the Humanities Bill for which so many had worked so long and so hard. Under the terms of this bill, an Advisory National Council on the Arts and a coordinating Federal Council on the Arts and the Humanities were set up, with funds of $10 million for each year, 1966, 1967, and 1968, with future authorization to be reviewed at the end of that time by Congress. Furthermore, a major objective of the legislation "is to stimulate private philanthropy for cultural endeavors and State activities to benefit the arts."

Hardly had the general rejoicing over this major victory begun to settle down a bit when a second announcement came along that vitally affected the first, and which even more directly affected the present, the immediate future, and the long-range hopes of every symphony orchestra in this country. This occurred on October 22 when the Ford Foundation announced an $85 million program for American symphony orchestras. This is the largest act of philanthropy in the arts by a single national agency. Its stated purposes are "to advance quality by enabling more musicians to devote their major energies to orchestral performance; to strengthen symphony organizations and enlarge the audience for orchestral music by permitting orchestras to increase their seasons" (and it is suggested that these increases may include more tours and more school, neighborhood, and suburban concerts); "to attract more talented young people to professional careers by raising the prestige and income of orchestral players."

This is not the time and place to go into detail about the provisions of the Ford Foundation program. But I must add that their program, vast though its total amount seems, is planned to take in, or rather to attract to, the fifty-eight major and metropolitan orchestras which it may affect, far more than the $85 million total mentioned, for it is a program in part made up of matching funds. If the program is completely successful, it will, on the basis of these matching funds, place a total of $165 million in the service of the orchestras it seeks to assist.

The timing of the Ford Foundation announcement, coming just after the signing of the National Arts Council Bill, undoubtedly had no small effect on the decisions of the Advisory Arts Council when it announced its grants for the first year of our new federal aid to the arts program. Knowing that this new financial aid was now in the works for our symphony orchestras, and for other, larger reasons as well, the Arts Council made no grants to individual orchestras. However, future grants under the federal program could very well take in various aspects of the orchestral situation, if the need seems pressing. At the moment, the great value of the federal legislation upon the symphony orchestras can be said to lie in its enormous moral power, a kind of suasive power that reminds the people of this country that the government regards the arts as a vital part of its total life. That this will do precisely what the wording of the bill suggests and encourage private donors to increase their own giving seems inescapable.

Another vital segment of the national picture is the slow but clearly increasing pace with which individual states are now moving into the field of official action in and support of the arts. State arts councils, until recently confined to New York State alone, now exist in Missouri and, if yet unborn, are gestating in a number of other states, or else exist in them already, under other less official titles. Clearly the machinery set in motion on the federal level is going to have its counterparts in many state actions. One of the most concrete evidences of this spreading interest in the arts is the number of centers of varying kinds that are now being provided under one aegis or another for the performing arts, in which music is always one of the chief ones.

For example, if one of the most vexing and demanding of all the questions now facing orchestral boards of trustees is: How are we going to keep these musicians employed for the forty-four to fifty-two weeks of the year that they are demanding, and which they, in simple justice, have coming to them? then one of the answers most regularly suggested is: Use them in the summer as well as in the winter. At the moment, all or part of the total membership of these orchestras are busy in the summer in some kind of outdoor music center: Boston, at Tanglewood; Chicago, at Ravinia; Los Angeles, at the Hollywood Bowl; Cincinnati, at the Zoo Opera; Denver, at the Red Rocks; San Francisco, at Stern Grove; the New York Philharmonic, both in Lincoln Center and in free outdoor concerts, which in the summer of 1965 drew over seventy thousand people to a performance of the Ninth Symphony of Beethoven played in Central Park.

An exciting number of new summer music centers are also moving onto the scene in various stages: the Detroit Symphony, which until 1964 had no summer home, now plays a busy series of concerts in conjunction with a full-scale, university-level summer music school at Meadowbrook, a few miles outside Detroit. And in the summer of 1965 the Philadelphia Orchestra, which had long played in the Robin Hood Dell in that city, forsook the Dell, where a second orchestra took over, so that the Philadelphia players were able to move to their new home at Saratoga Springs, New York. The Cleveland Orchestra has just finished an exhaustive survey of all possible sites within a 50-mile radius of that city and plans to open its full-length summer series in 1967, which is the same year that the National Symphony—the orchestra of Washington, D.C.—plans to move into its own new home in Columbia, Maryland.

Interestingly enough, all of these plans which I have just mentioned existed on paper or were well advanced in stages of building or of actual operation before the Ford Foundation made its dramatic act of generosity public. Yet it is entirely possible that without such a program some of these ambitious programs would have been impossible to carry out or would have foundered for lack of the necessary support after they had been begun.

Certain things are clear as a piece of exquisite Steuben glass—orchestral players were no longer willing or able to live on their salaries as musicians when those salaries were paid only part of the year; even with sold-out houses, every orchestra in this country was operating at a deficit which, annually, grew larger. That old source of financial support, such as a few large donors, was drying up; and that despite ever broader bases of public giving, rising costs were driving orchestra boards to desperate measures which could only succeed for a short time before disasters in various forms might strike. Only a few short years ago an article in *McCall's* magazine quoted such internationally known conductors as Fritz Reiner and Eugene Ormandy, certainly authorities on the subject, as saying that without new sources of support a number of leading American orchestras would have to go out of business permanently. And the chief source of that support was, at that time, thought to be the federal government.

Now the picture has changed, brightened, and while no one in the seats of the orchestral players is going to get rich, nor can orchestral boards relax for a moment their search for continuing contributions, there is a new and a different atmosphere in the orchestral world. Orchestral players have the assurance, backed by congressional legislation, that their country cares enough about them to want to help assure the future of their institutions; and they have the solid strength of a munificent private foundation which has realized not only their desperate plight but their inestimable value. They are regarded as essential to our cultural well-being in all seasons—when the weather is warm as well as when it is cold, and in rural surroundings as much as in our urban centers. When Leopold Stokowski several years ago told a special committee of Congress which was investigating economic conditions among performing artists that Congress should find ways of sending our symphony orchestras to regions in this country that had never seen or heard a symphony orchestra, he was making a suggestion that now takes on the aspect of prophecy, for our new legislation as well as the terms of the Ford Foundation grant makes it seem as if this kind of move on the part of some of our orchestras will become a reality.

In our technological advances in recent years, we have found ways of bringing superb *reproductions* of great performances of music to any who can manage the small cost of a phonograph recording. It is possible today to hear recorded examples of the whole history of music from pre-Christian days to today's music of chance and tomorrow's electronic score. However, we will not be judged a musical nation by the number of phonographs or recordings we buy, no matter how much we listen to them. But a part of our worth will be measured on those scales on which the late President Kennedy said "we will one day be weighed upon, the quality of our cultural life is of immense importance"; a part of that worth will be determined by the health of one of our finest musical possessions, our symphony orchestras.

Index